Tunes for Tots

by
Dr. Laverne Warner
and
Paulette Berry
illustrated by Carla Biggs Blackburn

Cover by Nancee Volpe

ISBN No. 0-86653-077-0

Printing No. 987654321

GOOD APPLE, INC.
BOX 299
CARTHAGE, IL 62321-0299

About the Authors

About Laverne Warner - Dr. Warner's experiences in teaching kindergarten, first grade and elementary music positions have led to the conception and development of **Tunes for Tots** for teachers of preschool through second grade. Her current position is with Sam Houston State University in Huntsville, Texas, where she is an Associate Professor in the Division of Teacher Education. She teaches undergraduate and graduate classes in early childhood education and an introductory course in elementary education. University teaching is a pleasurable activity for Dr. Warner along with her activities at the state and regional level in several professional organizations. She is President-Elect of the Texas Elementary Kindergarten Nursery Educators (TEKNE), has newsletter responsibilities in two organizations and has authored several articles which have been published in state and national journals. Rachelle (a niece, age 6) and Warner Matt (a nephew, age 4) are her loves and have tried a number of songs in this book.

About Paulette Berry - Mrs. Berry has fourteen years of teaching experience, five of which have been with four and five year olds. She received a B.A. from Lamar University (Beaumont, Texas) and an M.Ed. from Sam Houston State University (Huntsville, Texas). Paulette coauthored **Kindergarten Kapers**, published in 1975 by T.S. Denison and Company. She is presently teaching first grade in the Conroe Independent School District in Conroe, Texas. Her priorities in life include her husband Luther, her son Alan, a Dachshund named Little Bit and Bandit, the guinea pig.

About Carla Biggs Blackburn - Carla Biggs Blackburn received a B.A.T from Sam Houston State University (Huntsville, Texas) in the summer of 1981 and is currently teaching art in Hugh Springs, Texas. Private painting lessons and a considered art minor have given her a creative flair which carries over into her classroom activities. Her special talents include preparing a cozy home for a loving husband and irascible cat, cooking, writing poetry, gardening and developing unique teaching materials for use in her classroom.

TABLE OF CONTENTS

INTRODUCTION

A Note to Preschool Teachers

Using music in preschools is a traditionally accepted activity for teachers of young children. Music serves as a developmentally sound tool to use to communicate with youngsters in a uniquely effective way. Most children enjoy singing and will participate in musical experiences with enthusiasm and exuberance. Music spices up the curriculum and fills in at odd moments when teachers need to relate to children in a spontaneous way. It represents a natural part of the young child's life.

Many adults do not seem to realize how much value music has in a child's life or to what degree it provides for cognitive, physical, social and emotional growth. From a musical standpoint, children learn to match pitches, experiment with sounds and lyrics, and develop a sense of rhythm. Music promotes good listening skills and focuses on active participation, whether the child is singing individually or in a group setting. In some instances, music gives the restless child an opportunity to let off some excess energy.

When young children engage in musical endeavors, they are becoming more aware of themselves and their relationships with others. Most of the time, singing experiences occur as children become a part of a group of three, four, and five-year-olds who are like themselves. This added dimension to communication with others leads to an extended understanding of the child's world and how he fits into the environmental scheme.

Some children turn to music as a dependable inner resource which aids them during periods of stress. Creating songs to sing after the lights are turned off at night or developing lyrics about foxes, bears, or wolves, for example, may be alleviating some fears children are feeling at certain stages of their development. Other children may sing familiar melodies as a means of comfort when they are experiencing loneliness or anxiety about being in certain situations. In some rare cases, it may happen that children use music to express emotions they are unable to express in other ways.

Tunes for Tots is written for use with young children. Very few musical materials are available which are designed to assist the teacher of very young children. Most published series rely on traditional melodies which may or may not be appropriate to sing with young children. Song melodies are chosen because they are familiar to many adults who will be teaching them. The themes of songs are usually related to seasonal or holiday topics. Because of these two facts, a majority of the musical selections teachers choose are unfitting for children's immature voices and creative, spontaneous singing is not encouraged nor enhanced.

Music for young children should be developed with their abilities and musical needs in mind. Children's voices are limited in range (about five to six notes from C to G or A above). Asking a young child to sing notes above this range may cause distortion of sounds for the child's musical "ear" as he attempts to match tones which he is able to sing. Just as a four-year-old needs practice in other curriculum areas to become competent, he needs practice in the musical areas as well. But this practice needs to be within his capacity as a beginning singer. If children are not allowed to rehearse songs that are comfortable to them and suitable for their young voices, they soon become frustrated and give up trying to do that which is too difficult. No wonder many adults exist today who believe they cannot sing because they have a feeling of inadequacy about musical matters.

This book contains musical selections which preschool teachers can use with confidence with young children. All of the songs are written in order to be comfortable for young voices. Most of the songs utilize a range of four to six notes and are within the octave from B below middle C to B above. If this material is learned first and practiced with consistency, then children will not encounter problems when moving to more difficult songs at a later age.

Most teachers with limited musical study will note that the songs are written in familiar keys (C, D, F and G). Chords for each song are included if the teacher chooses a guitar or autoharp as a musical accompaniment. Rhythms are also simply noted. Quarter, eighth, and half notes are used consistently with a few scattered sixteenth notes to add zest. For the teacher who feels totally inadequate about music, the songs can be used as poems or fingerplays as various curriculum areas are studied. Both the musical and nonmusical teacher will want to add a variety of motions to the songs to assist children in understanding conceptual ideas and participating in basic movements.

The themes of the songs are categorized in the following areas:
(1) Getting Acquainted, (2) Body Awareness, (3) Holidays, (4) Seasons and Weather, (5) Community Helpers, (6) Transportation, (7) Animals, Insects and Birds, (8) Counting Songs, (9) Just for Fun. The song lyrics are based on areas of study usually considered appropriate for preschool children. Activities to accompany the songs are included to aid the beginning teacher in planning musical experiences which correlate with other areas of the curriculum. These activities are not all inclusive, however, and should spark the thinking of teachers of young children and spur them to higher levels of creative teaching.

Children, too, need to be encouraged to expand on these songs. Even preschool youngsters can and will create their own musical compositions and movements if the teacher and environment encourages them to do so. Listening to children as they sing or perform will give the teacher insight into the level of understanding individuals have for music. Youngsters learn from one another and will likely become motivated to develop their own musical skills by watching and imitating others.

Some teachers may want to go beyond the scope of this book to expand on basic musical concepts. When this occurs, the following musical concepts are those which are best to concentrate on: (1) matching pitches, (2) discriminating among high and low pitches, (3) defining the direction of melodies (whether melodies move up or down), (4) understanding steady beats, (5) discovering rhythms move fast or slow, (6) learning to recognize quarter notes (and later eighth notes) and (7) notating children's compositions.

The most important component in developing musical experiences for three, four, and five-year-olds is the teacher's attitude. Teachers need to be positive when approaching musical activities and remember that all children do not have the same musical talents and backgrounds. A good attitude will promote interest in and enthusiasm for music. The result will be youngsters with merrier outlooks on the world and healthier concepts about their musical abilities.

GETTING ACQUAINTED

One of the major hurdles a child faces in a new school is getting to know his peers and his teachers. Most children adapt easily and readily to the learning setting, but support from the teacher is essential in developing satisfying interrelationships within the classroom environment. Children will respond favorably to songs which request them to say their names or select others who are their friends. Stimulating interaction among preschoolers will foster a relaxed, cordial classroom environment which teachers and students alike will find acceptable and enjoyable.

Suggested concepts to be developed in this section include:

* The child can learn to share in a group situation.
* The child can learn to become a part of a group.
* The child can make new friends.
* The child will become aware that friends can be all ages, races and sexes.

SONGS:

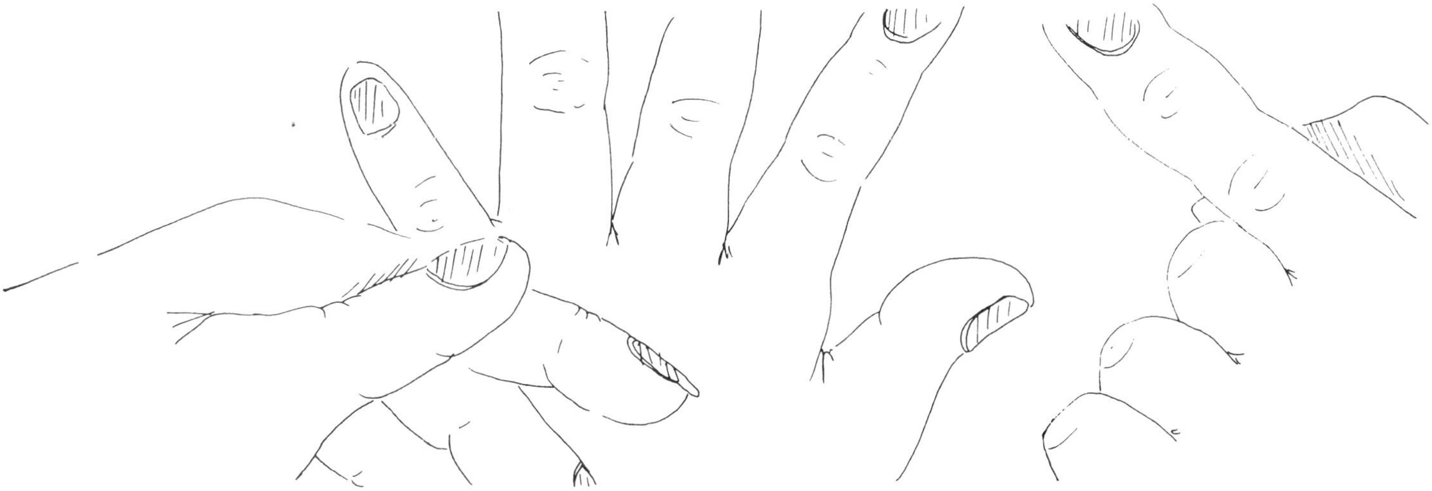

Won't You Be My Friend?

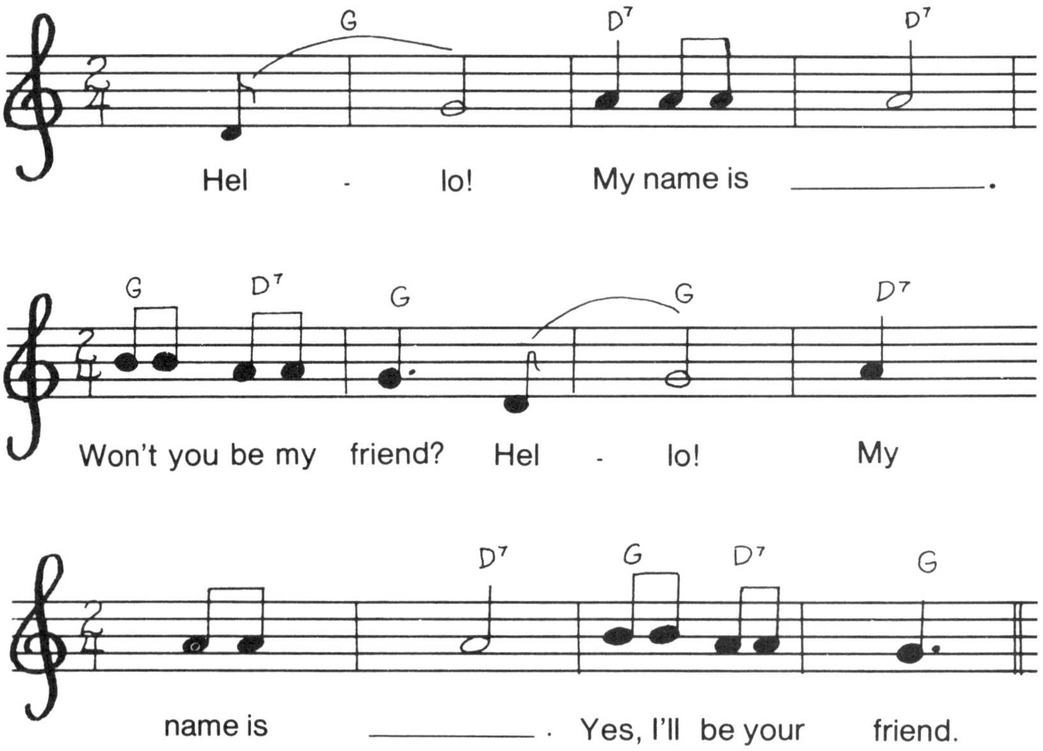

Choose a friend and play in a center with him or her during playtime.

Have the children draw portraits of their best friends. The teacher can label and display the pictures in the room.

H-E-L-L-O

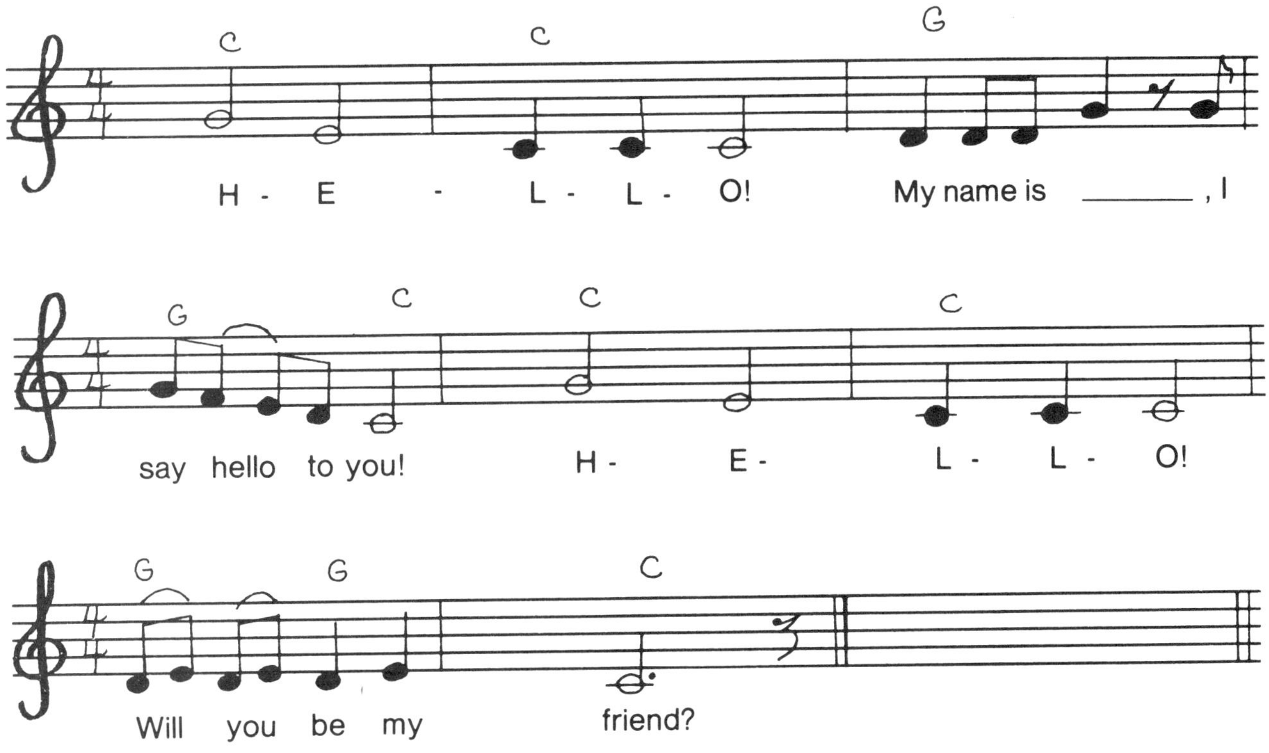

Turn the song "Hello" into a game. After the children know the words of the song, form a circle. Choose one child to begin. He will stand in front of another child and sing the first phrase. The friend will answer by singing phrase two. It is suggested that the teacher let the children volunteer for this game as some children may be too shy to participate.

On a large heart-shaped piece of paper, have each child draw himself with a good friend. Label the picture "Me and My Friend." Or use finger paint and ask the child to place his or her handprint on one half of the heart. Likewise, a friend places a handprint on the other half of the heart.

Round and Round

Play a game entitled "Round and Round." Children are seated in a circle. One child begins the game by walking or skipping around the circle until the third phrase of the song. Then he chooses a friend to join him in the game. Each time the song is sung, each child chooses a friend for himself.

When the class has a new member, encourage the children to help the new child become a part of the group.

Good Morning to You

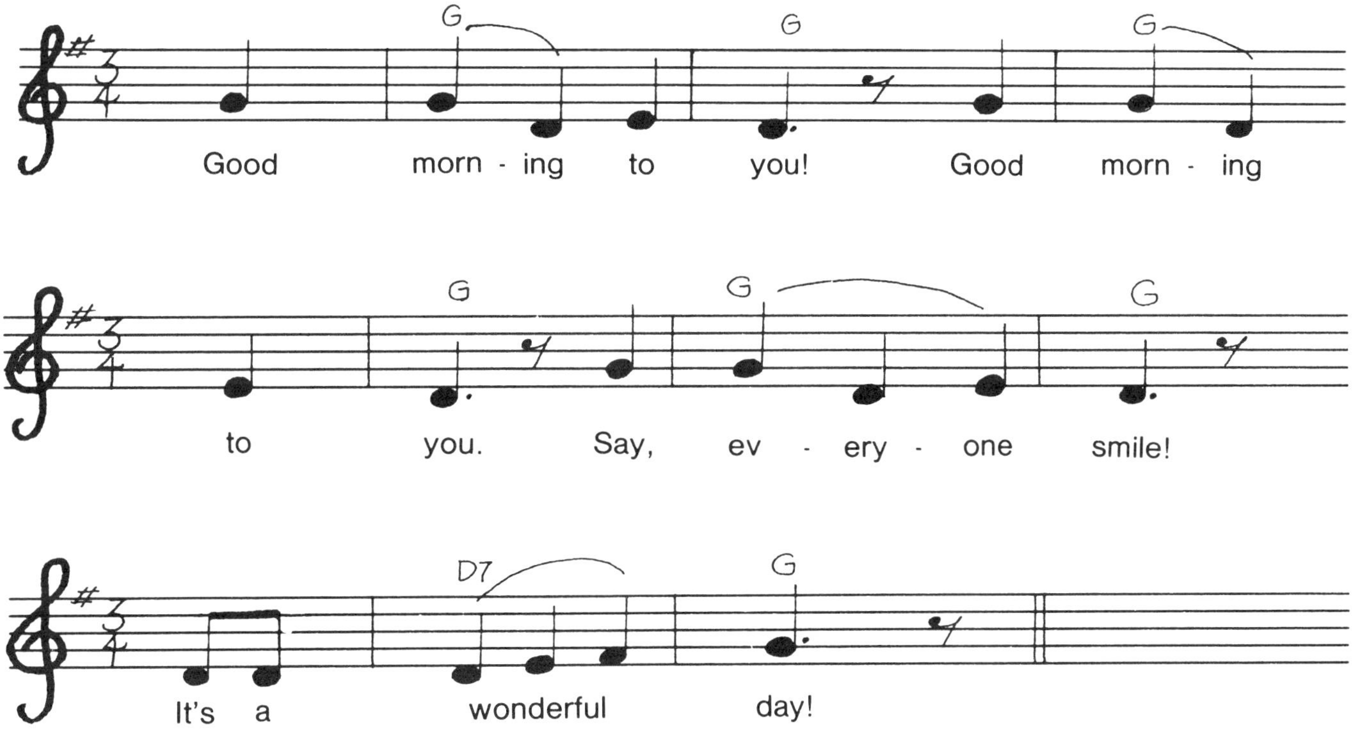

Have the class discuss the topic "Who are our friends?" Encourage the children to consider such people as the janitor, secretary, principal, cafeteria workers, etc.

Take the class to visit some of their school friends such as the secretary, principal, etc.

Monday Morning

Have a class dramatization to discover how to welcome a new student to the classroom.

Substitute another weekday name for "Monday" when singing the song.

Check to find out who in the group is absent.

As a class project, make a giant card for a classmate who is sick. Each child can draw, paint or color something on the card and sign his name.

BODY AWARENESS

Individualism is never more apparent than in preschoolers. Children talk, laugh, play, interact and communicate in uniquely important ways. They want to be accepted for themselves and not for the person adults expect them to be. They are spontaneously active and eagerly diligent in all activities they choose. Occasionally, they are even more observant than the adults who supervise or direct them.

Clarifying emotions and labeling body parts become a method to help children be increasingly aware of themselves as individuals. A child will stand taller and smile broader if he knows that the adults in his life care about the needs he has as an active, growing person.

Suggested concepts to be developed in this section include:

* Each child is unique and special.
* Each child can use parts of his body to express himself.
* Each child needs to express himself physically by moving, bending, stretching, etc.
* Each child needs to be free to express his emotional feelings.

SONGS:

Follow Me

After the children have learned this song, give individual children an opportunity to lead the group in other "Follow Me" activities (clap and clap, stomp and stomp, nod and nod, bend and bend, etc.). The children will enjoy thinking of their own creative suggestions.

Can You Do What I Do?

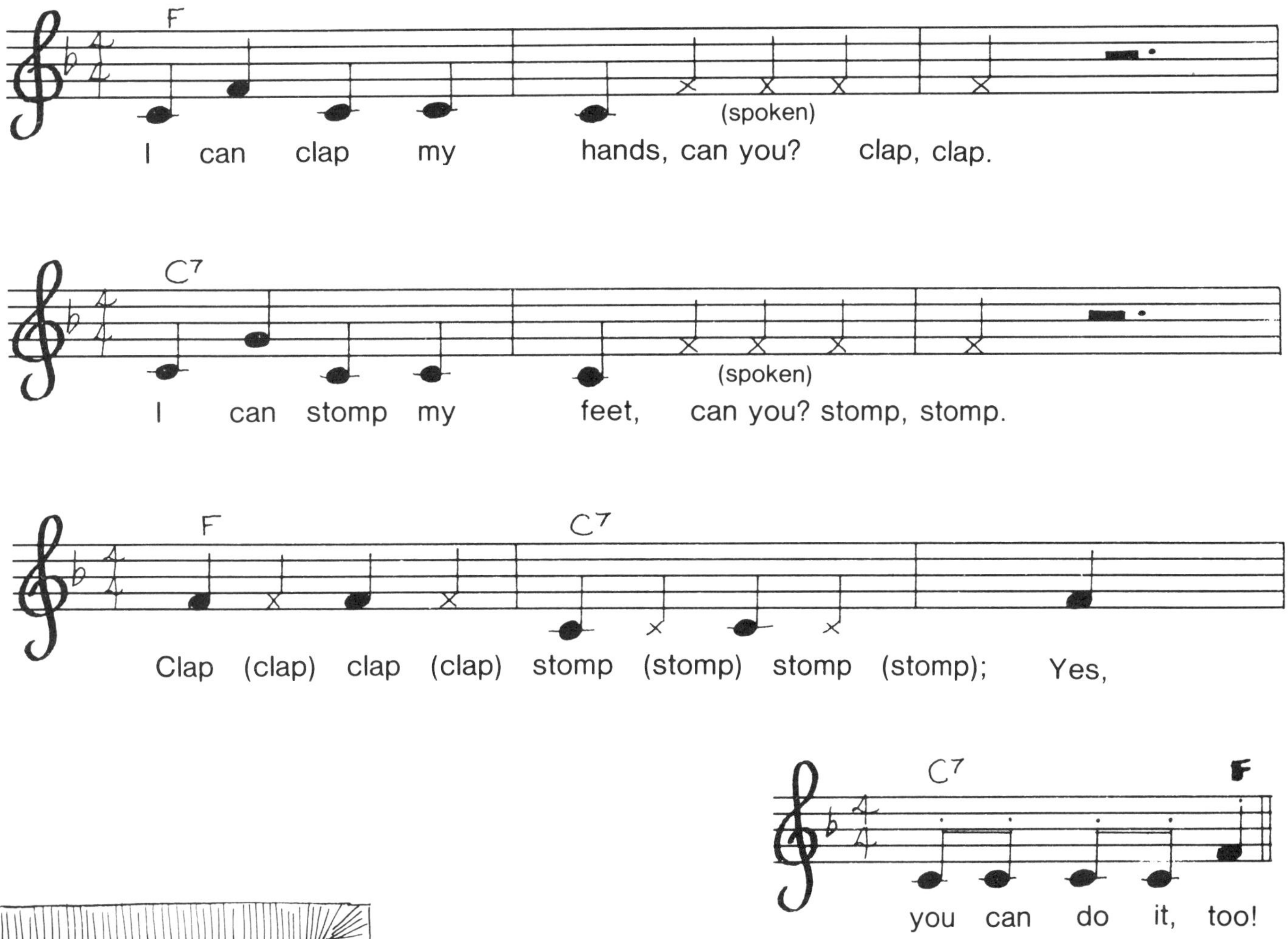

Play the "Do What I Do" game. Choose a leader to stand inside the circle of children. The leader makes a movement for the other children to imitate. The children may take turns being leader.

Introduce the words **imitate, mimic** and **follow the leader** to the children. Tell them that the words mean the same thing as **do what I do.**

Hand, Hand, Fingers, Thumb!

Make clown finger puppets and let the children manipulate them so that they appear to dance like clowns.

Finger Puppet

front view

back view
(Adjust to fit wearer's finger)

Use tagboard with this puppet. Fingers are inserted through the holes.

Feelings

Show pictures of children with various expressions. Encourage the children to discuss the feelings shown on the faces. Let the children relate examples of their feelings. Perhaps the children can dramatize situations of fear, happiness, etc.

Let the children finger-paint and talk about the touch sensations they feel.

Bend and Reach

Lead a discussion about how tall the children are when they reach and how small they are when they bend.

Record each child's height and weight at the beginning and end of the school year.

Talk about the differences in height between children and adults. Invite a male in the school to visit and compare his height with those of the boys in the classroom. Use the same experience with an adult woman.

Help children become aware that athletes spend much of their exercise time bending and reaching in order to become more agile.

The Wiggle Song

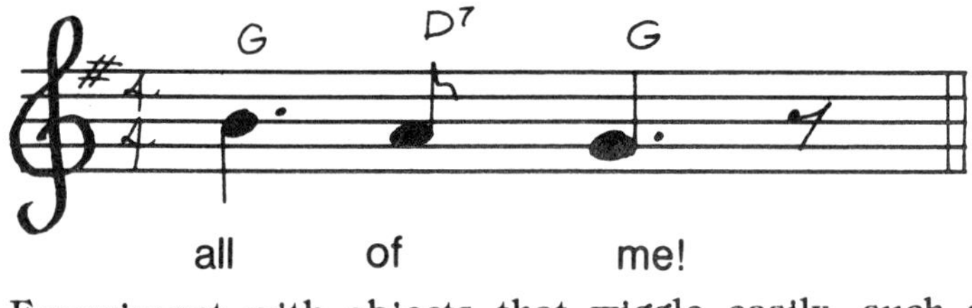

Let the children express themselves by wiggling as each body part is named.

Experiment with objects that wiggle easily, such as a bowl of Jell-O, a Slinky, a marionette or night crawlers. Focus on vocabulary development by using the words **shake, jiggle, quiver, squirm** and **shimmy.**

Exercise!

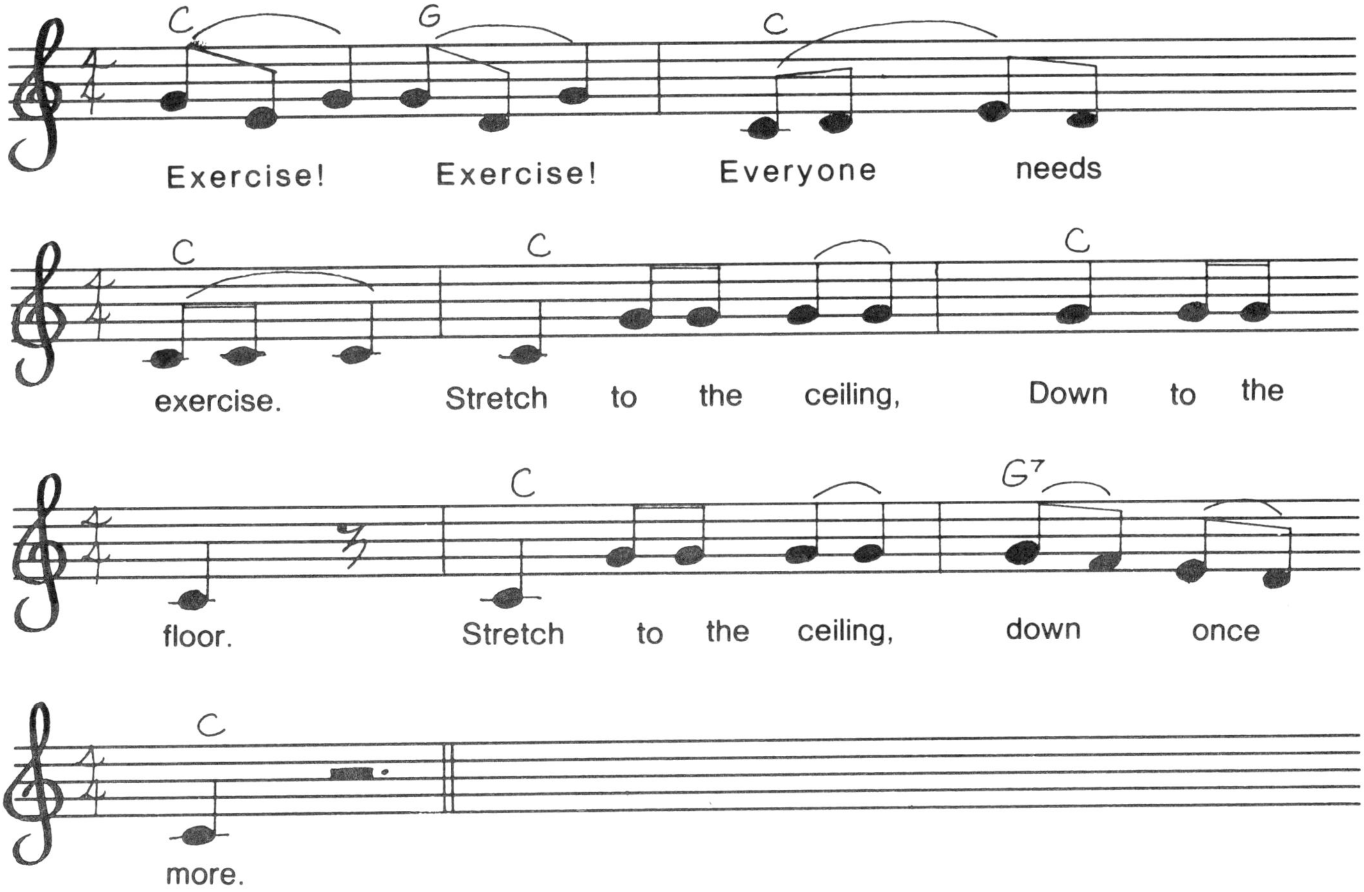

Provide tumbling mats and professional teachers to help children practice simple gymnastics.

Review the song "Bend and Reach" shown on page 19.

Develop a classroom scrapbook. Ask children to collect pictures from home which show how persons of all ages exercise to keep fit.

S-H-H-H-H-H!

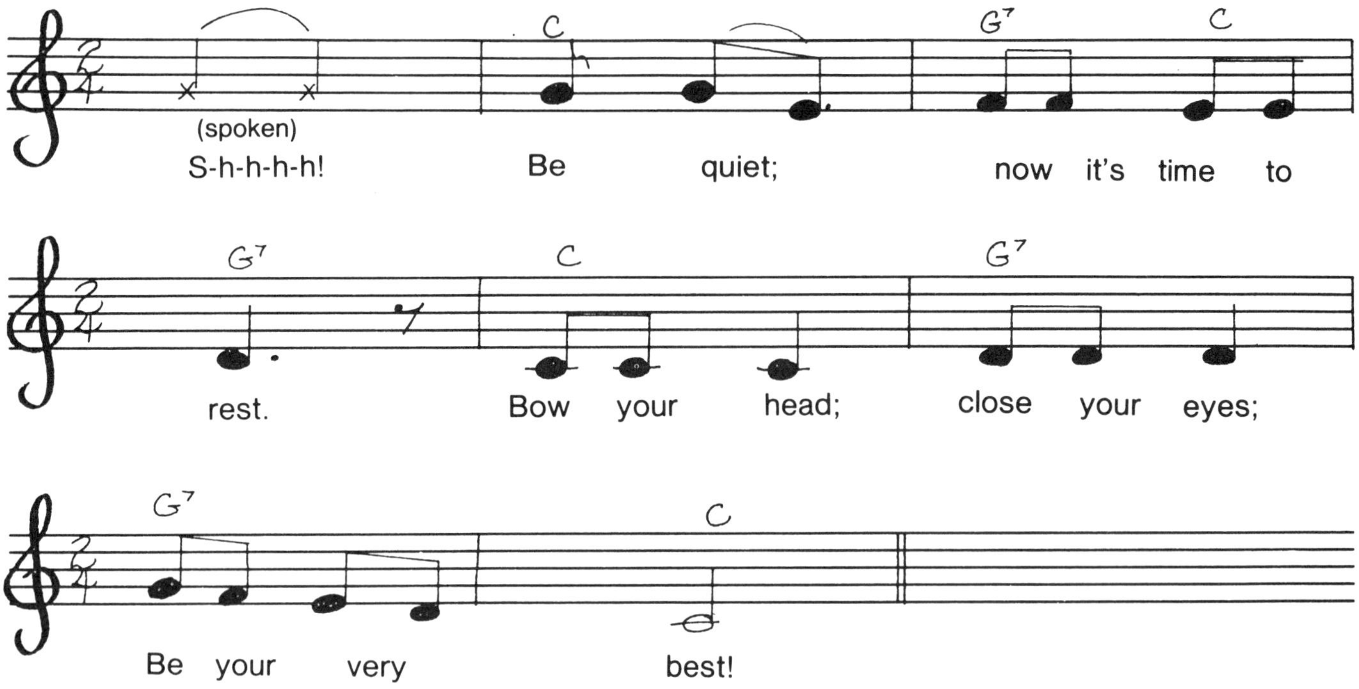

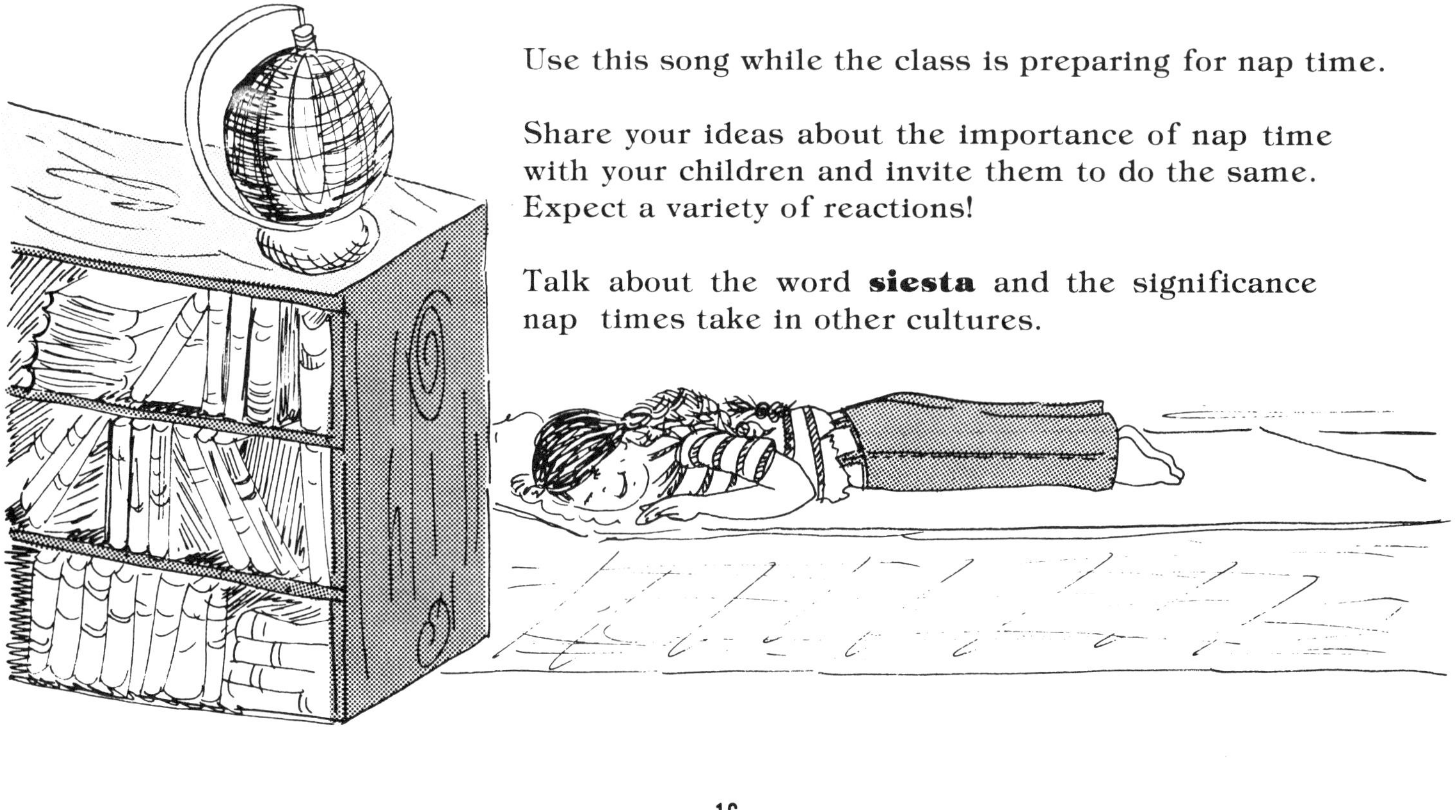

Use this song while the class is preparing for nap time.

Share your ideas about the importance of nap time with your children and invite them to do the same. Expect a variety of reactions!

Talk about the word **siesta** and the significance nap times take in other cultures.

Listening Ears

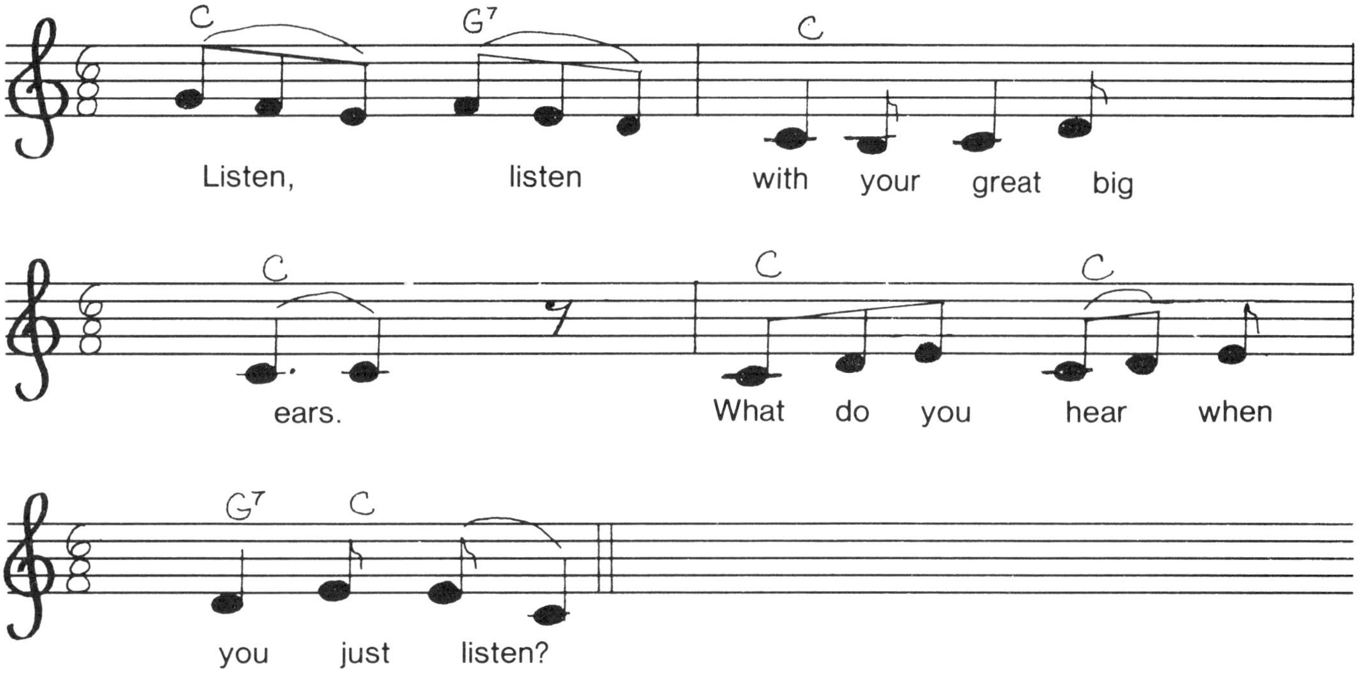

Make a puppet with big ears. Let this be a listening puppet. The children may go to the puppet and talk to him whenever they feel like it. The end result may enhance language development in the shy child.

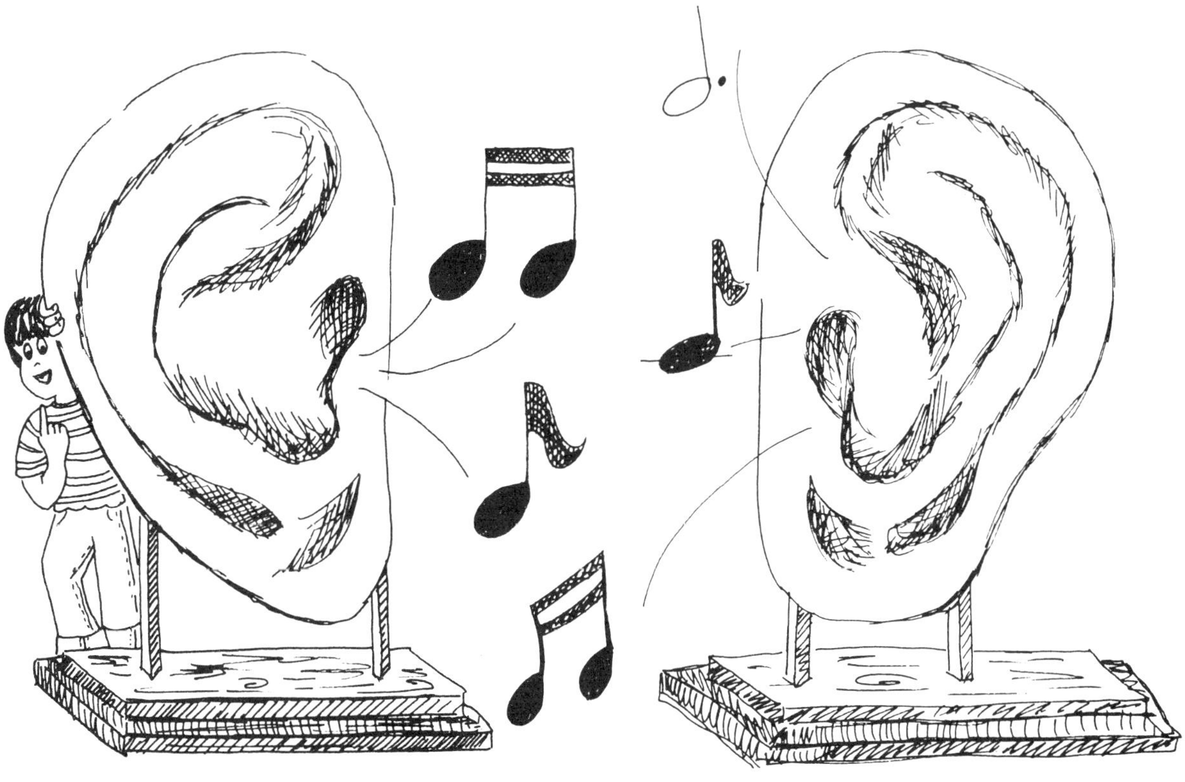

Take the children on a nature walk. Ask them to listen to the sounds around them. It is suggested that the children close their eyes and listen to the sounds.

Special Things

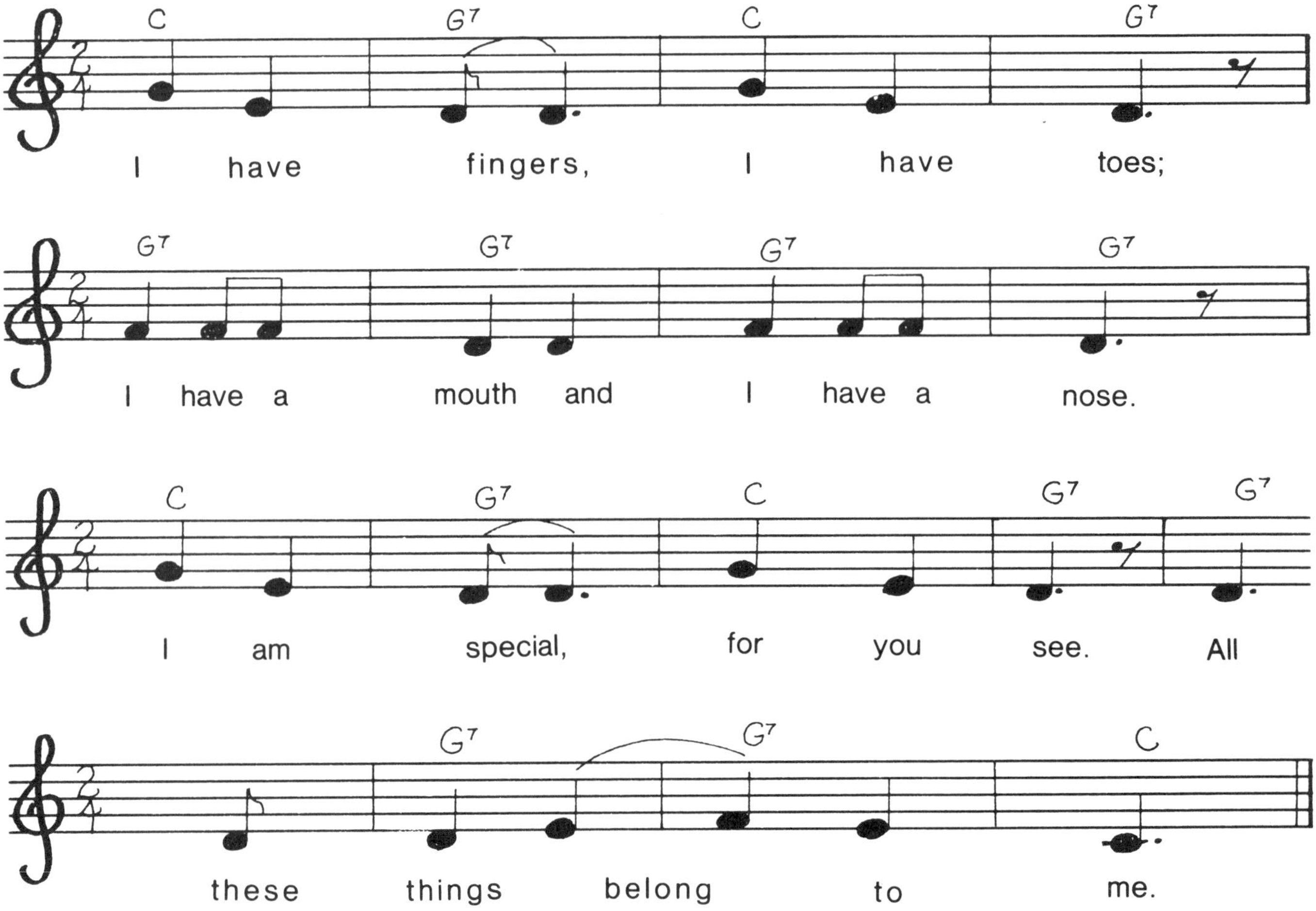

Each child should create an "I'm Important Because" badge to wear in the classroom and take home at a later time. Assist the child in making statements about himself which help him feel unique.

The teacher (or an older child) may trace around the child's body on butcher paper. Allow the child to fill in with crayon or paint.

Learn a second verse:

I am friendly, I have "heart";
I like to share and take my part.
I am loyal and so true.
I'll be a friend just for you!

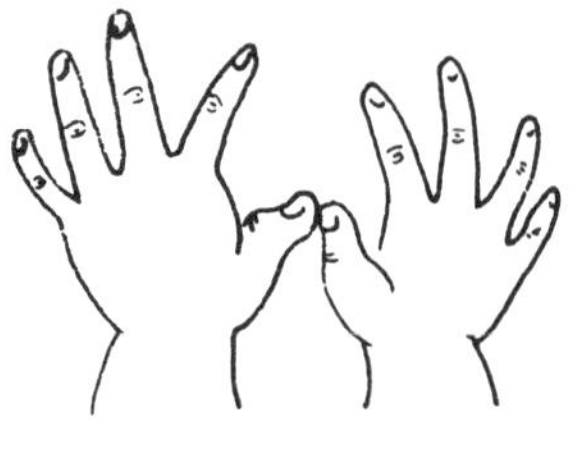

S-M-I-L-E

Talk about the importance of smiles and demonstrate that smiles can be contagious.

Make a class collage of smiles which have been cut from magazines the teacher has brought from home.

Instruct the child to smile at one person as he leaves the classroom for home.

If I Were a Bee

Display each child's baby picture on one side of a bulletin board and his current school picture on the opposite side. Have the children match the pictures by connecting them with string.

Talk about animals children observe in their environments and discover why each is special. Urge the children to try out various animal sounds and movements.

Make comparisons between baby animals and adult animals. Notice that certain changes take place as they grow older.

Holidays

Holiday periods are exceptionally enjoyable moments for children. The anticipation children feel is evident when they are caught up in the hustle and bustle of seasonal events. Incessant questions occur as children ask about Santa's arrival, for example, or the advent of Halloween happenings. The wise teacher will make adequate provisions for several activities to keep youngsters engaged in purposeful behavior. Individual art activities, group projects (such as dramatizations and murals), fingerplays and stories are appropriate and necessary.

Holidays also focus on family plans and outings with friends. The child will be curious about customs and traditions set up by his own family and those of his friends. Sharing sessions within preschool classrooms give the child a glimpse into the lives of his peers. What an excellent way to help children find out about others.

Suggested concepts to be developed in this section include:

* Holidays have both religious and secular meanings.
* Each holiday has certain symbols associated with it.
* Each holiday has its own festivals and traditions.
* Holidays are times when family and friends get together.

SONGS:

Boo!

Cover a lollipop with a soft white tissue to make a ghost. Add facial features with black markers. Children can make their ghosts "fly" while singing the song.

Place sheets of newspaper (the advertisement sections are excellent for this activity), glue and black construction paper in the art center. Children tear or cut ghosts out of the newspaper to glue on the black paper. The black-and-white result is effectively "Halloweenish."

Hee, Hee, Hee!

Invite children to come dressed in Halloween costume and parade through the building.

A school-sized chain of costumed children may be formed. When the kindergarten (or preschool) children parade through the first grade classrooms, then these children become a part of the parade. Each group of children joins the Halloween march and continues through the classrooms until they have returned to their home spots.

It's Halloween!

A suitable Halloween project would be one where children make a "treat" box to take to the children's ward or a local home for the aged. The box can contain such things as cookies the children have made and iced. Get permission from home officials to have a Halloween Serenade by the children.

Children enjoy making popcorn and many educational opportunites arise as they listen, smell and taste the finished product. Try sprinkling grated cheese over a pan of popcorn and putting it in the oven for five minutes at 350 degrees. Yum!

Who Do You See on Halloween?

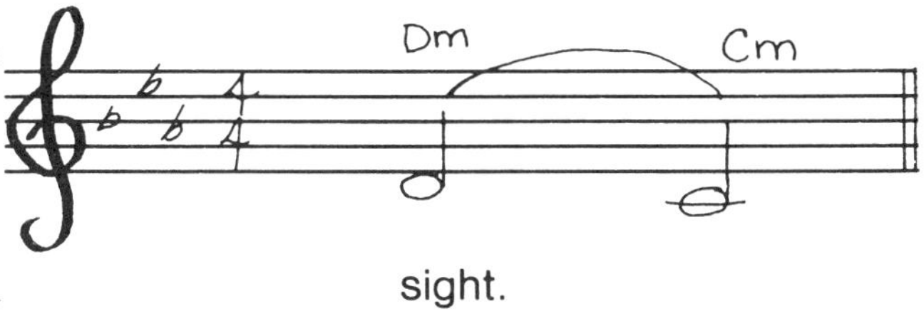

Experiment with musical instruments to discover ways to make this song seem "spookier" than usual.

Play a "Guess Who" game by allowing individual children to "hide" under a ghost's sheet. Children have to guess who is the ghost. Make the game more difficult by having several children "hide" at the same time.

Turkey Gobbler

Place turkey-shaped cookie cutters in the play-dough center.

Record each child making "gobble-gobble" sounds. Play the entire recording on another day to see if the children can identify their own imitations.

Visit a turkey farm if one is nearby.

We Are Thankful

Assemble a booklet entitled "Things I Am Thankful For." On each page of the booklet, the children can draw pictures of things they are thankful for.

After the booklets are complete, ask the children to share their favorite pictures with their classmates. Encourage them to conceptualize orally what they think the word **thankful** means. The teacher may want to share the reasons she is thankful.

Pick a Big Pumpkin!

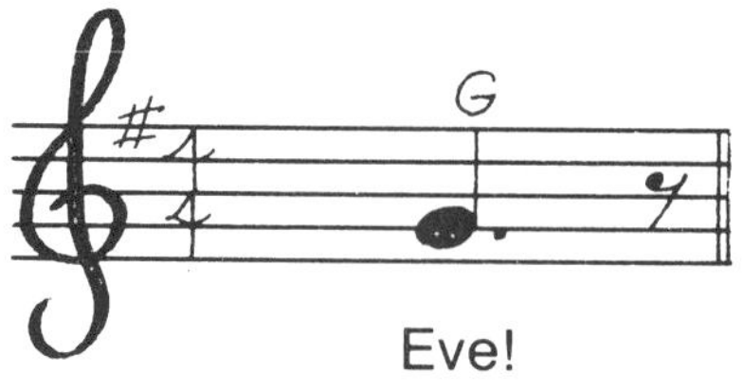

Visit a truck farm that grows pumpkins. This is an opportunity to teach a science lesson on plants (those that grow on a vine, bush, tree, etc.).

Talk about the various meanings of the word "patch." Vocabulary development is important for the young ones.

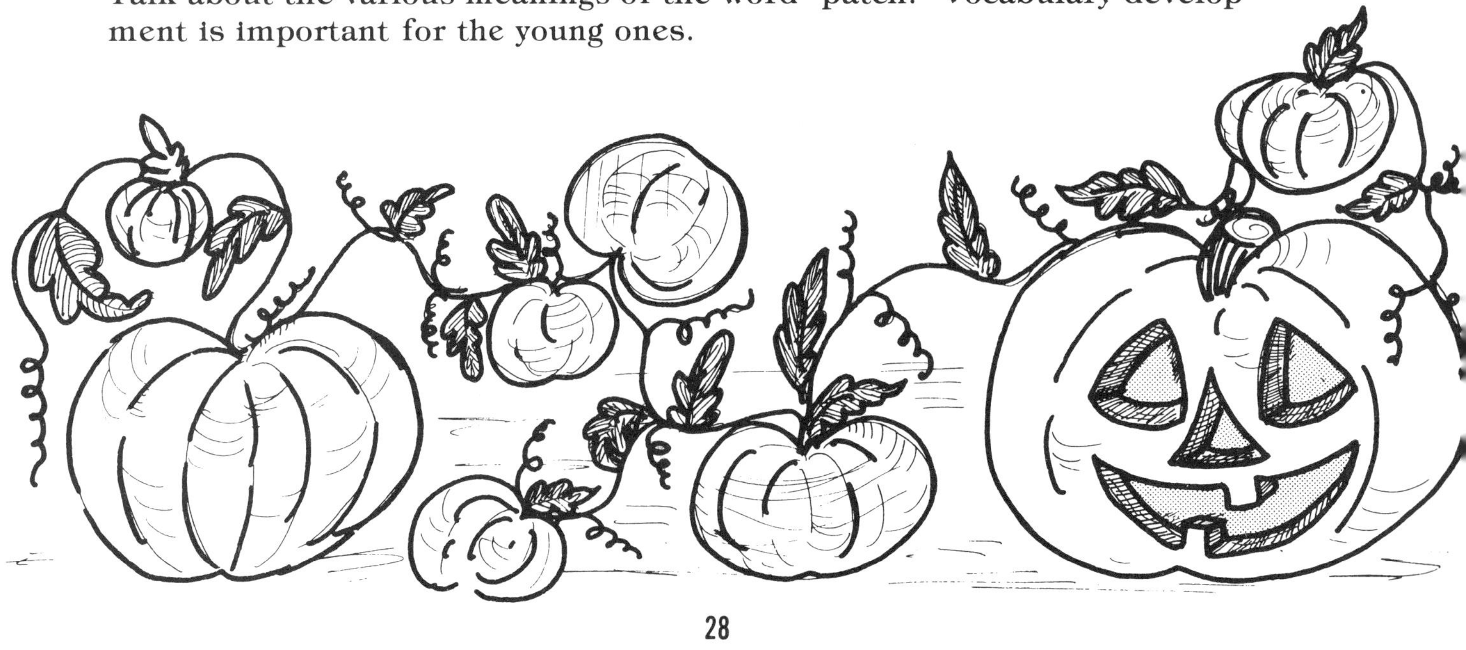

Indian Brave

Make Indian headbands, paper bag vests and Indian bead necklaces for children to wear. Assist children as they pick out an Indian name for themselves. Wear the Indian outfits they have made and call them by their Indian name on "Indian Day."

Headbands - Cut construction paper bands to fit the child's head. Cut out "feathers" to glue to the band.

Vests - Cut armholes in the sides of a large grocery sack. Cut up the center of the bag to form an opening and cut a neck in the bottom of the bag.

Sleigh Bells

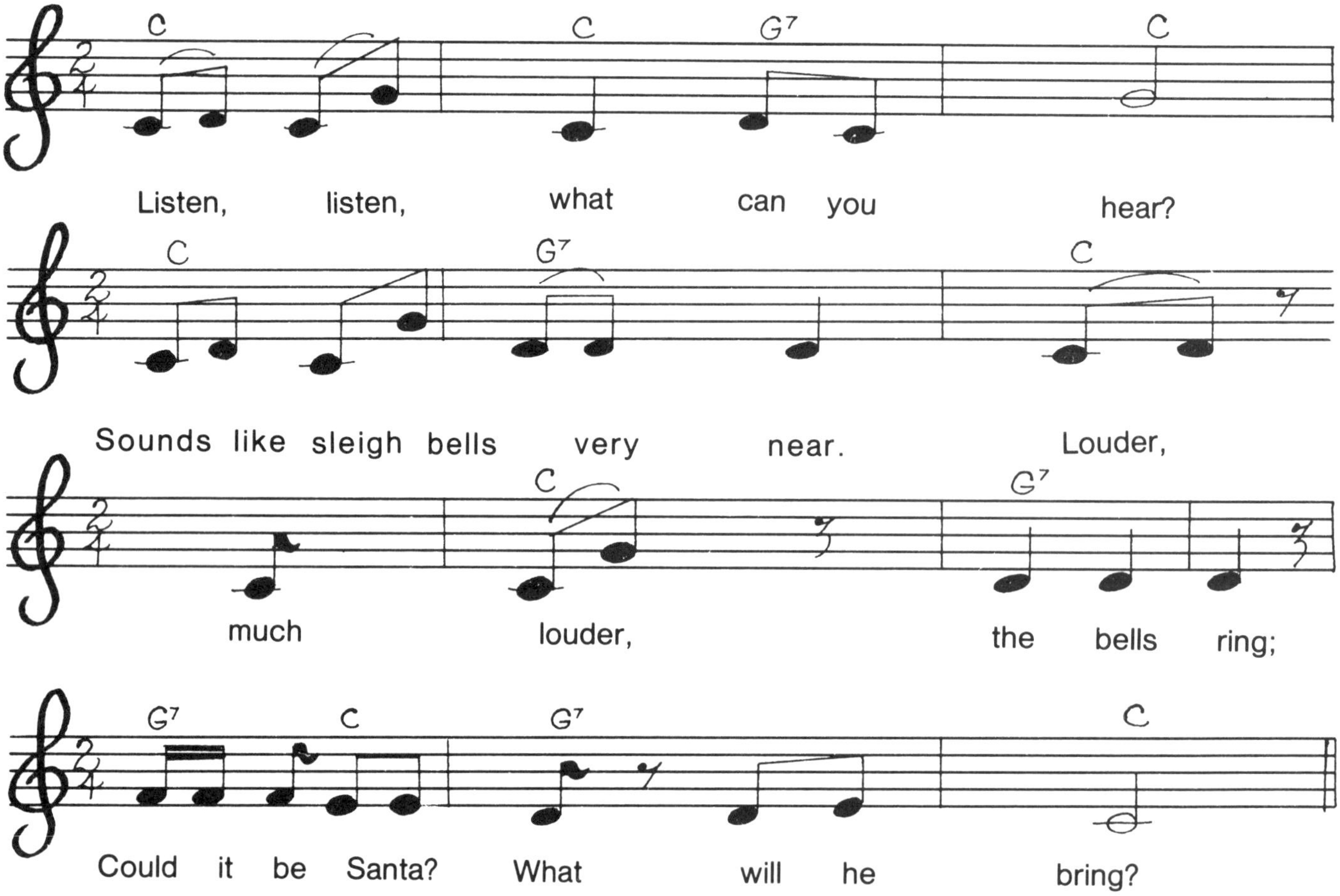

Attach small bells to an elastic band. The children can wear these "bracelets" and keep rhythm as they sing "Sleigh Bells."

Bring a harness to school which has bells attached to it. Demonstrate how the bells ring as horses pull the sleigh.

Christmas Bells

Cut a bell shape from green, red or white felt. Using a pan of tempera paint in desired color, have each child dip his hand into the paint and press his handprint onto a felt bell. These bells may be mounted on heavy paper, dated and framed as Christmas gifts.

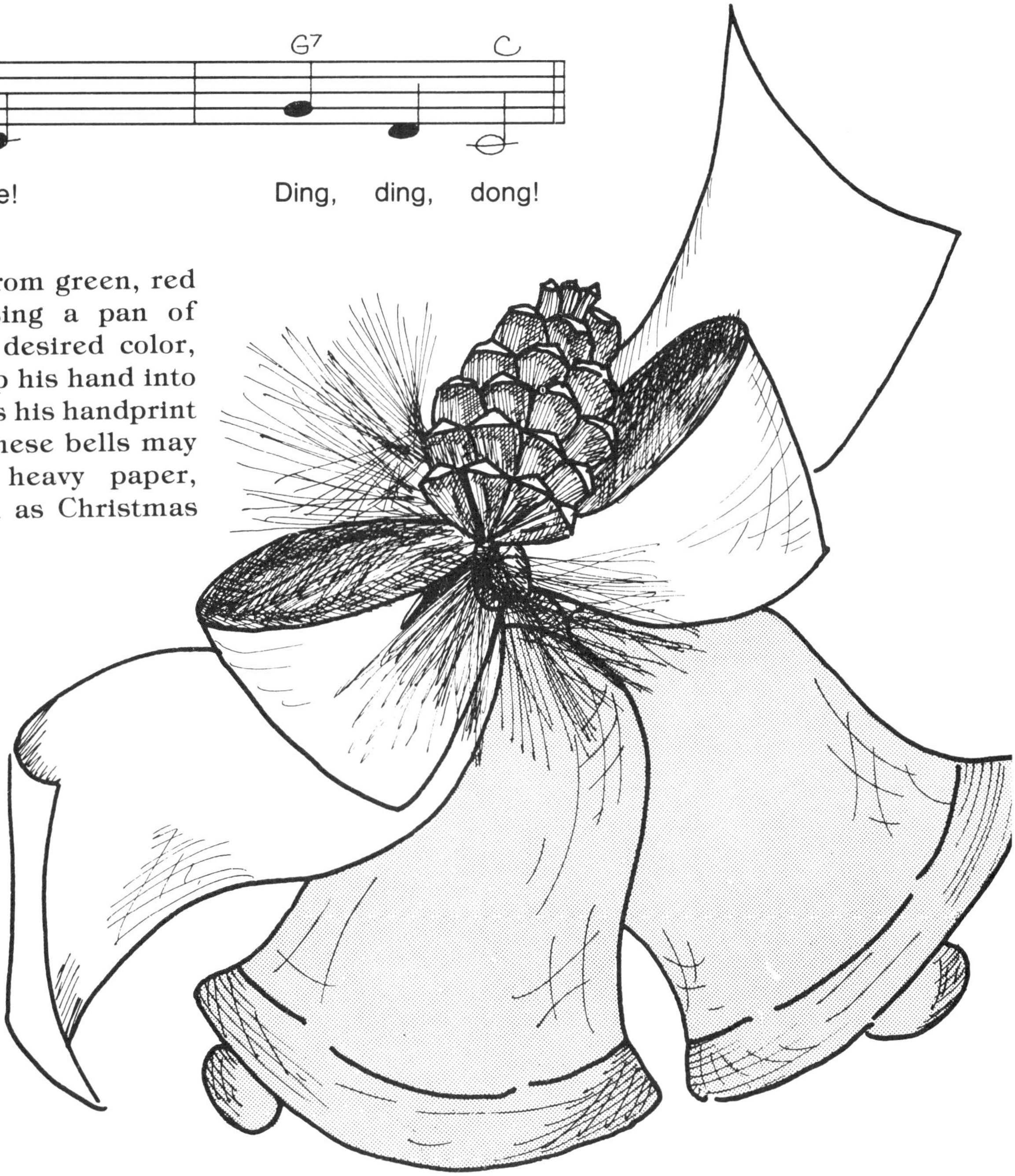

Santa

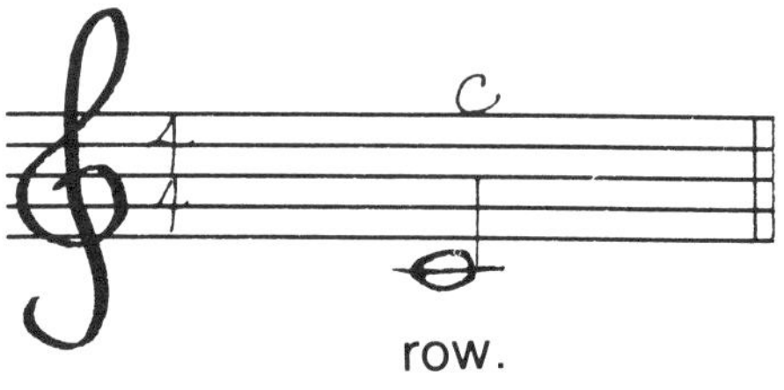

Wrap several gifts with Christmas paper. Let the children shake them to guess the surprises inside the packages. Gifts can be opened later and placed in classroom centers for everyone to share.

Bring merchandise catalogs from home to place in the art center. Ask the children to prepare a "Christmas Wish Book" by cutting out pictures of toys and other items they want for Christmas to glue or paste in the "Wish Book."

Wise Men

Provide special time for children to act out the birth of the Baby Jesus.

Bring a manger to the classroom and fill it with clean, soft hay. Talk about the animals that might have helped the young baby go to sleep at night.

Give children time to talk about the various Christmas "traditions" they have in their own homes. Be prepared to support the child who may not have pleasant Christmas memories.

Be My Valentine

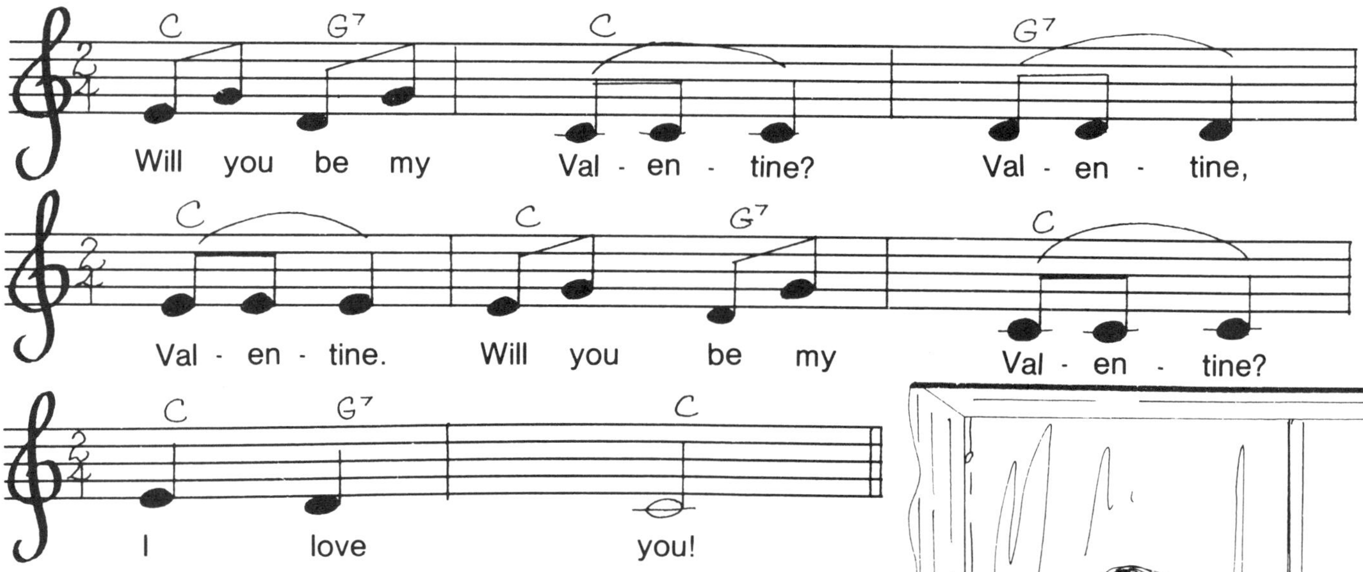

Let children stuff precut and sewn red felt hearts to make a pin cushion. Some children are able to use large needles and sew their own hearts together. Let them experiment at will!

Sing "Be My Valentine" to each child at "line-up time" at the end of the school day. Tap each child as the verse is sung so that he may get his coat and line up at the door. Make sure everyone has a turn!

The Leprechaun

Give each child a construction paper shamrock, a large sheet of paper and glue or paste. Let him attach the shamrock to the paper and then use crayons to fashion a "leprechaun" using the shamrock as the body.

Have several strips of various shades of green paper in the manipulatives center. Observe children as they seriate the strips of paper from **darkest** to **lightest** shades. Give the children who are having difficulty with the activity some basic instruction about differences in shades of colors.

Easter Basket

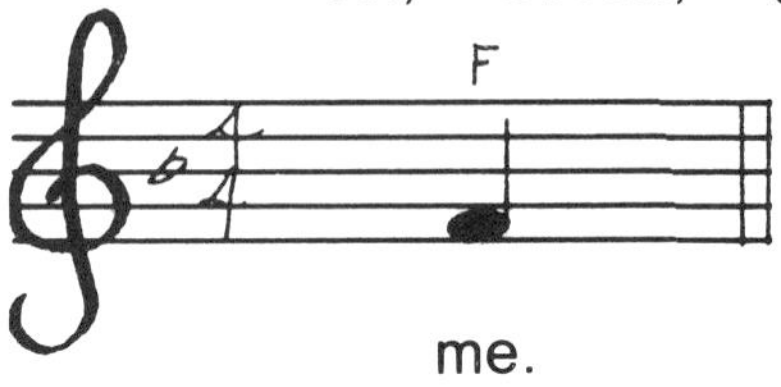

Visit a chicken farm. Purchase some eggs and discover in the classroom how eggs can be cooked.

Make Easter baskets. These can be made from plastic strawberry containers, bottoms of gallon milk cartons or bottoms of oatmeal containers. Use creative ideas for decorating the basket.

I Wish I Was a Bunny

Decorate plastic eggs as rabbits.

Make a rabbit by covering a paper cup with cotton balls. Add extra balls where the head is located. Complete the rabbit by adding paper ears, eyes and whiskers.

Easter Morning

Dye and decorate eggs for an Easter egg hunt.

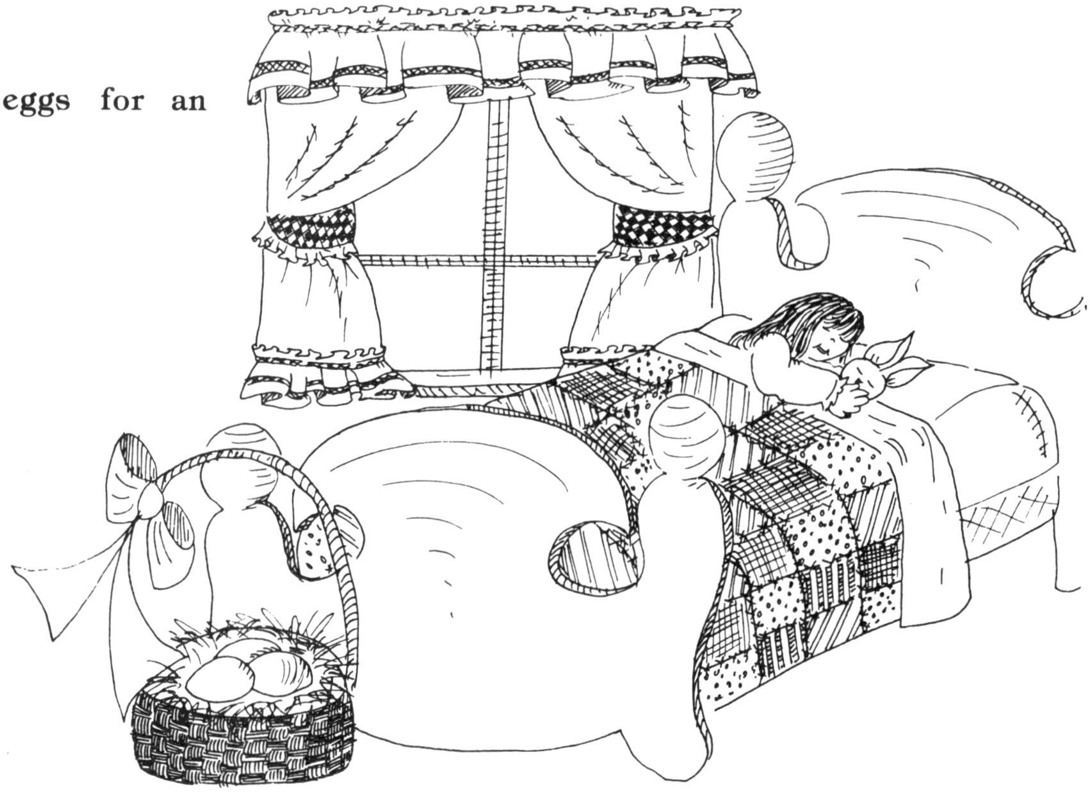

Mother

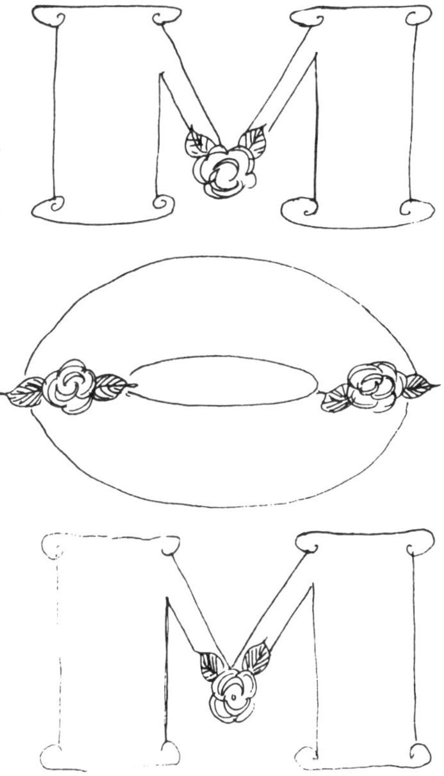

Have each child draw a picture of his mother. Give the child an opportunity to dictate to the teacher or teacher's aide what a mother is. Later type the statement on a strip of paper and attach to the picture.

Seasons and Weather

One of the earliest concepts children attempt to understand is the change in the weather because of seasonal factors. "Why does it get hot?" or "Why does it snow?" they ask. They are intrigued by rain, thunder, sunshine and seasonal changes. At times, they are even frightened by abrupt or bizarre weather changes.

The preschool teacher focuses on seasonal events and day-to-day weather occurrences as a topic of natural interest. The study of weather gives the preschool teacher an opportunity to introduce basic charts and graphs to children. Simple time concepts and comparison of daily weather factors are also concepts which can be developed. It seems that seasons and weather have such a profound influence on children and adults alike that singing about these topics should prove to be a delightful experience for children.

Suggested concepts to be developed in this section include:

* There are four seasons in the year.
* The earth takes on certain physical characteristics during each season.
* Particular weather conditions are common to each season.
* People take certain precautions when the weather is inclement.
* The media helps keep us informed about the weather.

SONGS:

Changing Leaves

Develop a classroom mural. One group of children can draw and paint a tree trunk and branches while another group goes on a nature walk to collect leaves. Talk about the colors of the leaves as they are glued to the mural.

Falling Leaves

Dramatize leaves falling to the ground.

Plan a science lesson about the differences between deciduous trees and evergreen trees.

Send the children on a scavenger hunt in a nearby park or wooded area to find the most beautiful fall leaves they can find. Use the leaves the children find to develop a classroom bulletin board entitled "Our Favorite Leaves."

L-L-L-L Goes the Wind

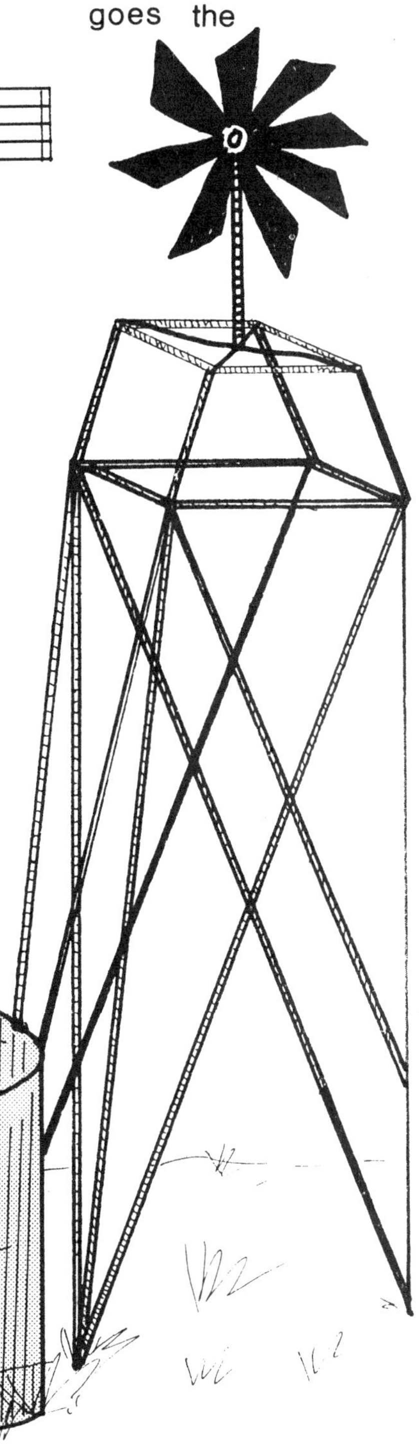

Find a book in the school or community library about windmills.

Listen to a tape of wind blowing.

Have a class discussion about the various ways wind is helpful to man (scatters seeds, flies kites, dries clothes, sails boats, keeps people cool during summer, etc.).

Pitter, Patter

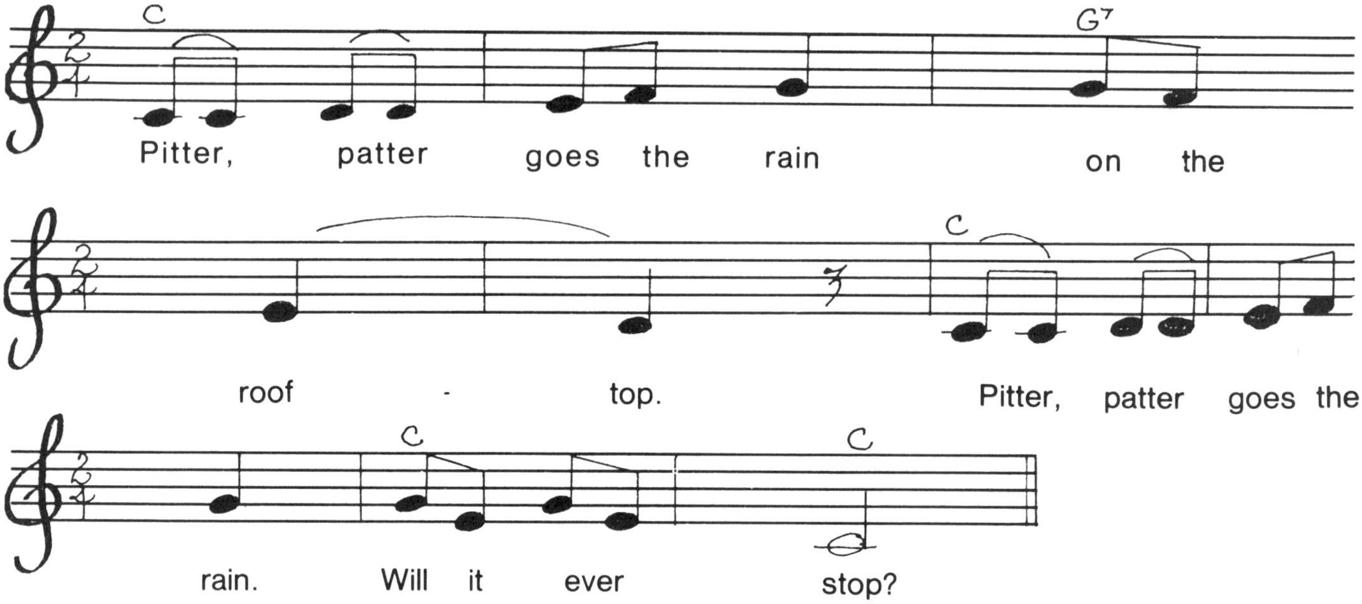

Measure and record rainfall over a one to three-week period.

Splish, Splash

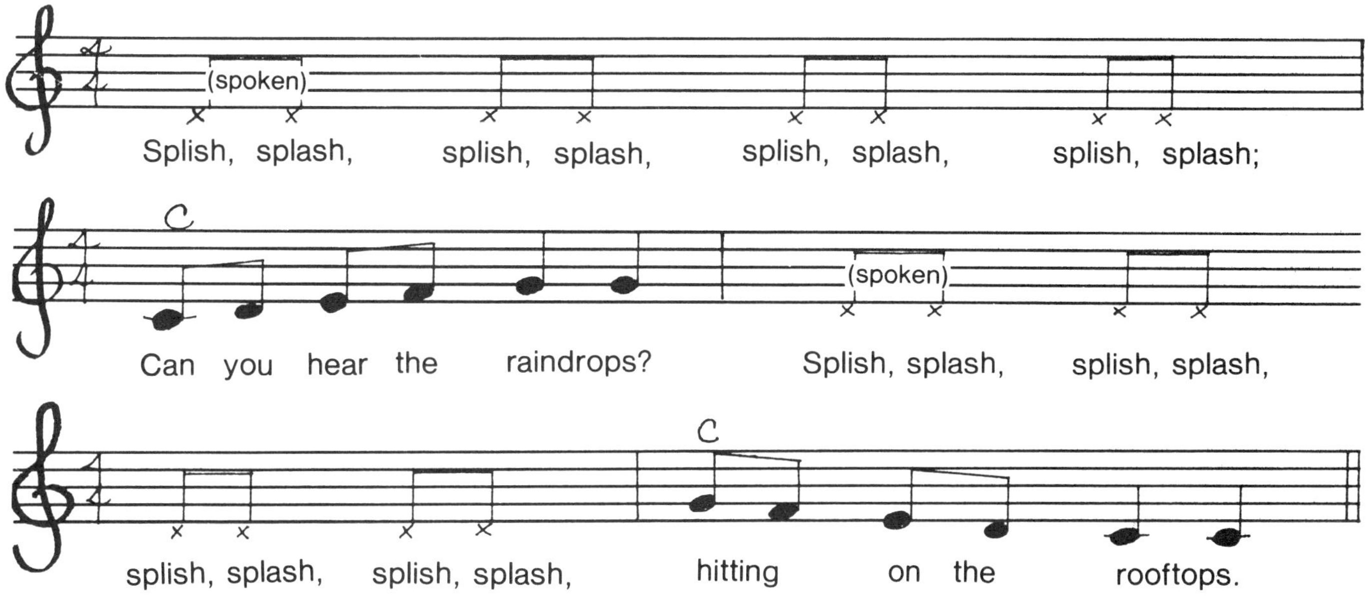

Make a swishing sound with the palms of your hands by moving them back and forth in time to the music. Speak the "splish-splash" words in this song in a very hushed voice.

The North Wind

Collect a box full of clothes which are usually worn at different seasons. Ask the children to choose the clothing appropriate for a chilly day.

Thunder

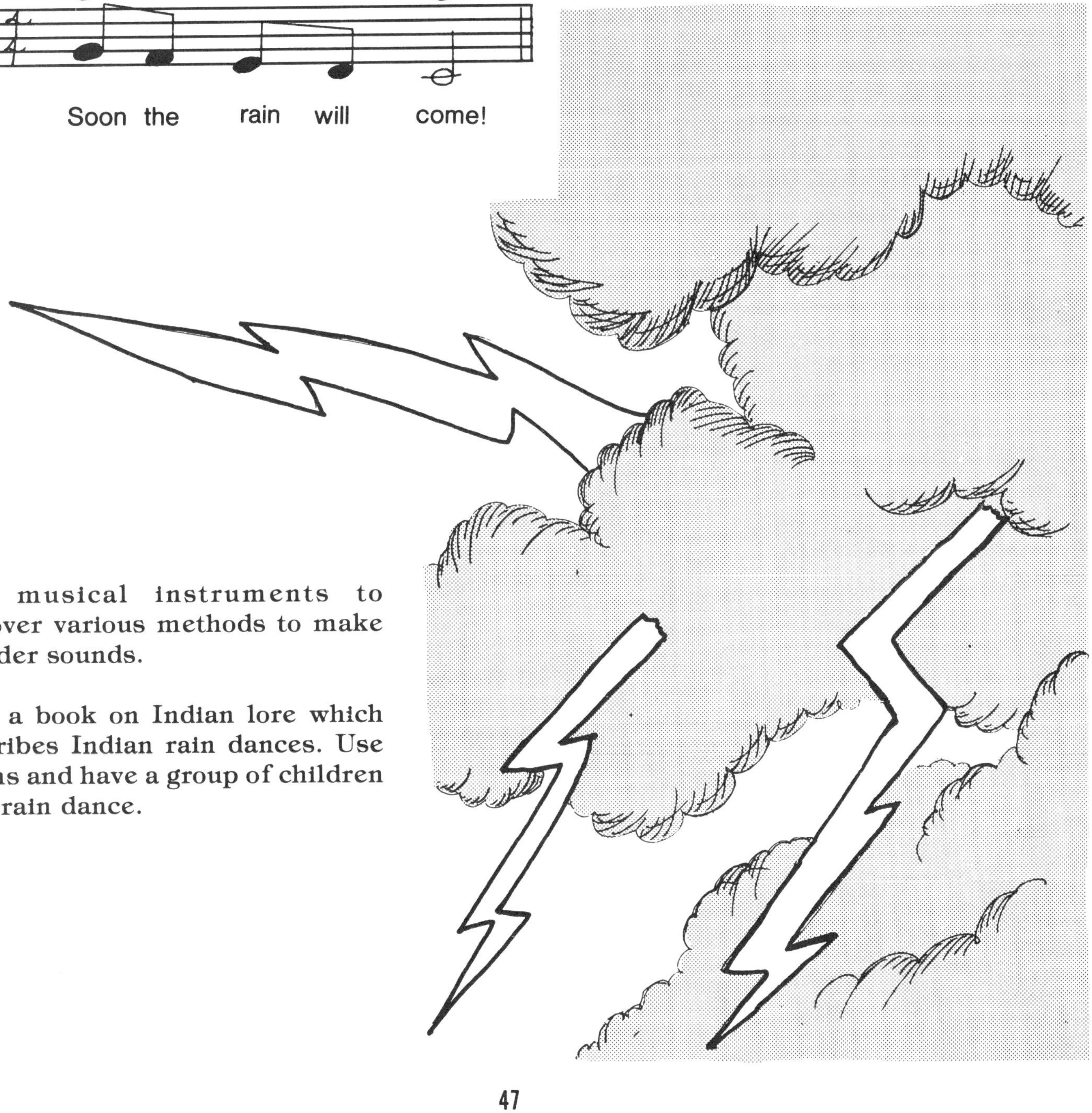

Use musical instruments to discover various methods to make thunder sounds.

Find a book on Indian lore which describes Indian rain dances. Use drums and have a group of children do a rain dance.

The Rainbow

Observe a rainbow. Then let children create their own rainbows with water colors or tempera paint.

Cut crepe paper streamers using the colors mentioned in the song. Instruct the children to use rainbow-shaped movements over their heads as they sing.

Spring Is Here

"Plant" a bare limb in a bucket with plaster of Paris. Use bright-colored tissue to make tiny blooms and leaves to attach to the branches.

The classroom tree can remain in the room the entire year. Change the spring blooms to appropriate items which relate to each new month (such as pumpkins in October, hearts in February and shamrocks in March).

Talk about the changes in nature which occur during the spring season.

A Growing Plant

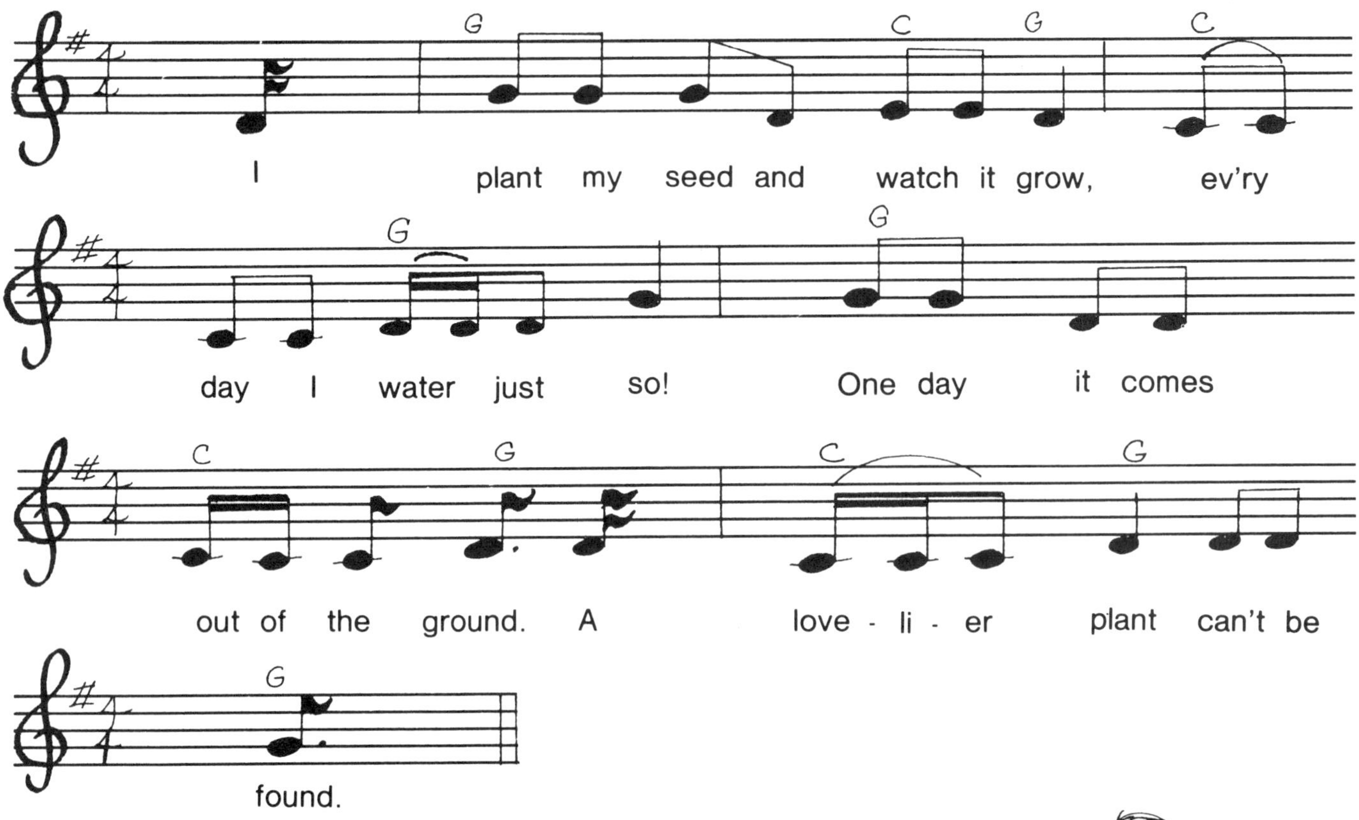

Plant flower seeds and record the growth on a chart.

Use empty seed packets to plant a make-believe garden on a classroom bulletin board.

Seed packets can also be used to develop a matching game for the manipulatives center. Observe children as they match the packets that are alike or categorize those that are similar in some way (i.e., **flowers, vegetables, fruits,** etc.).

Summer Has Come

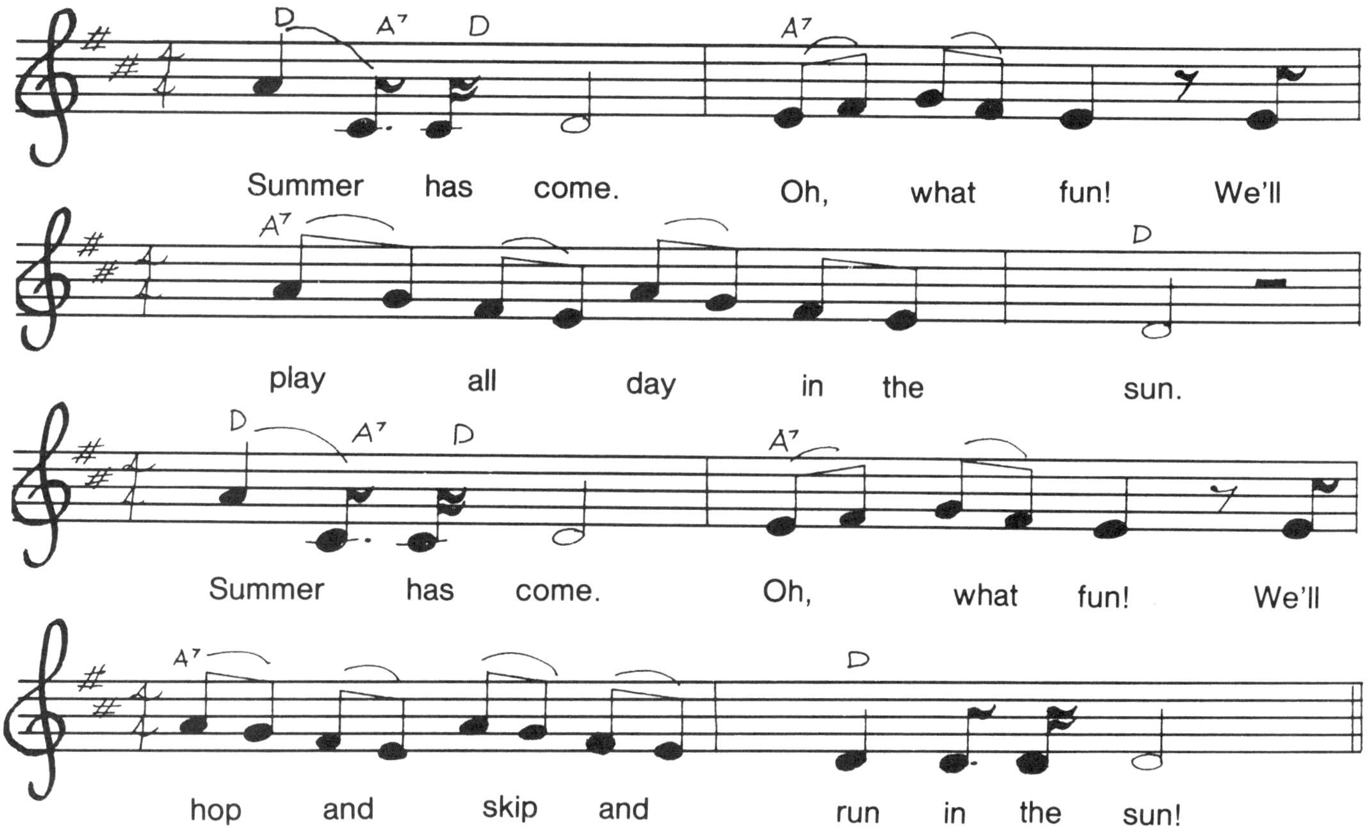

Let the children tell about their planned summer vacations in a sharing session. Correlate their proposed trips with a bulletin board in the room which shows suggestions for interesting places to visit.

Prepare one center in the room which children can use to display favorite artifacts they have collected on recent trips.

Good Morning, Clouds

COMMUNITY HELPERS

One of the questions adults ask children is "What do you want to be when you grow up?" Children then respond based on glamorous aspects of a career they have observed. Many times their job choices are limited to a few community positions which happen to be more frequently encountered in public settings. In addition, young children are especially puzzled about what one does when one "goes to work."

It becomes the duty of the preschool teacher to share knowledge about a number of community helpers with children. This information will stimulate preschoolers to develop a greater interest in the work of adults they meet in a variety of situations. They can also benefit by being encouraged to ask questions and imitate community roles that are revelant to their lives.

Suggested concepts to be developed in this section include:

* Community helpers play an important part in our lives.
* Community helpers are our friends.
* Adults serve in the community in different roles.
* Community helpers are interdependent.
* Roles change as society changes.

SONGS:

Mr. Policeman

Ask a policeman to visit the classroom. Accent the positive services policemen provide for citizens.

Yippee, Yippee, Yea!

Cut a brand on a potato. Provide several "branding irons," tempera paint and manilla paper for children to stamp their brands. A child's initial makes a personalized brand.

Invite a cowboy to visit the classroom. Ask him to demonstrate rope tricks. Later, allow the children an opportunity to "rope" items on the playground. A bale of hay is nice to rope, but it's better to put it outside in order to avoid a big mess in the classroom.

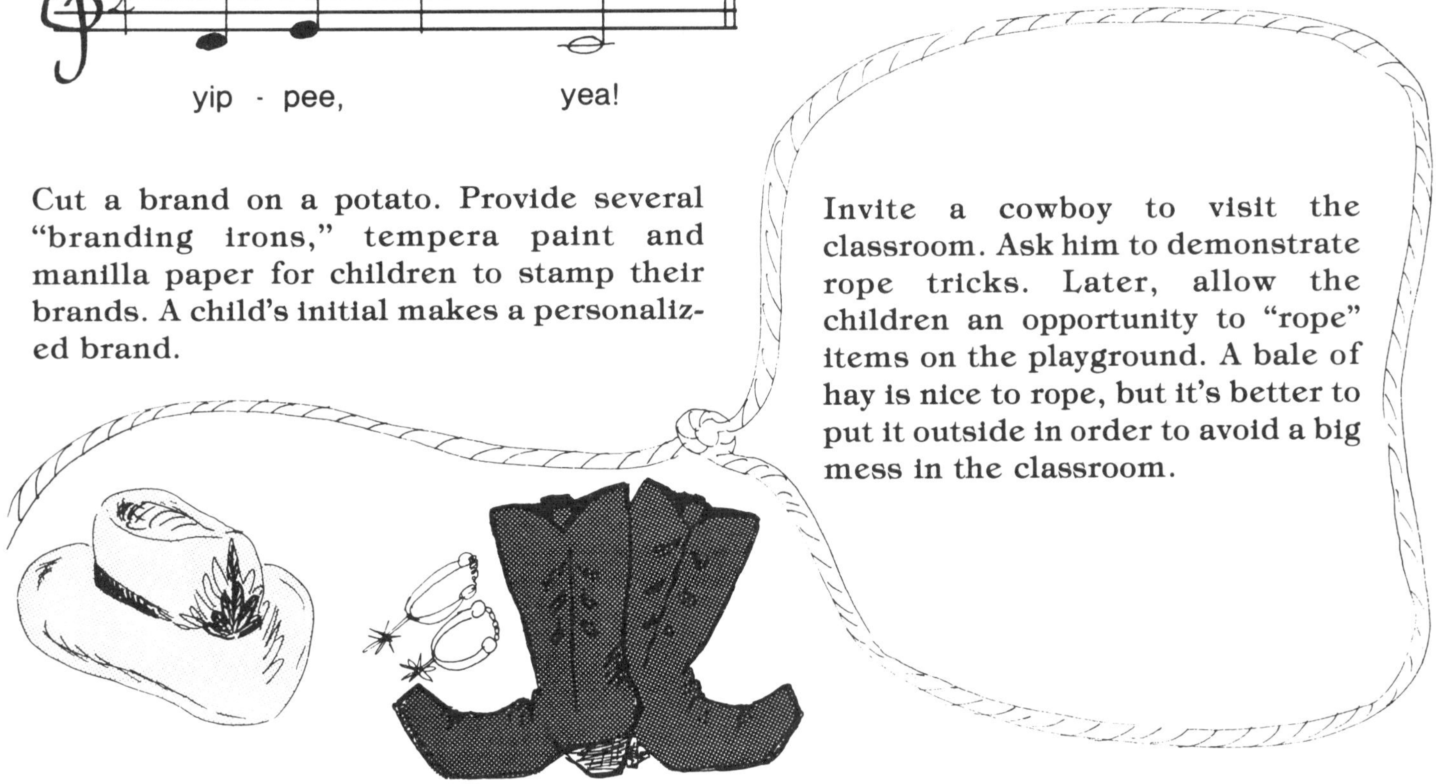

Mr. Weatherman

Appoint a "junior" weatherman for each day to be responsible for dialing a weather chart to the appropriate weather condition.

The Postman

Dramatize being a postman. A classroom post office can be organized prior to Valentine's Day. Children can deliver their valentines to the post office and the postman can deliver them to the post-office boxes. Plan boxes for special people in the school (the principal or director of the school, the custodian, or the librarian, etc.).

Carpenter

Make a visit to a cabinet shop or a nearby construction site.

Supervise the children in assembling a birdhouse to put on the school playground.

Discuss safety rules to follow when using carpenter's tools.

The Moving Van

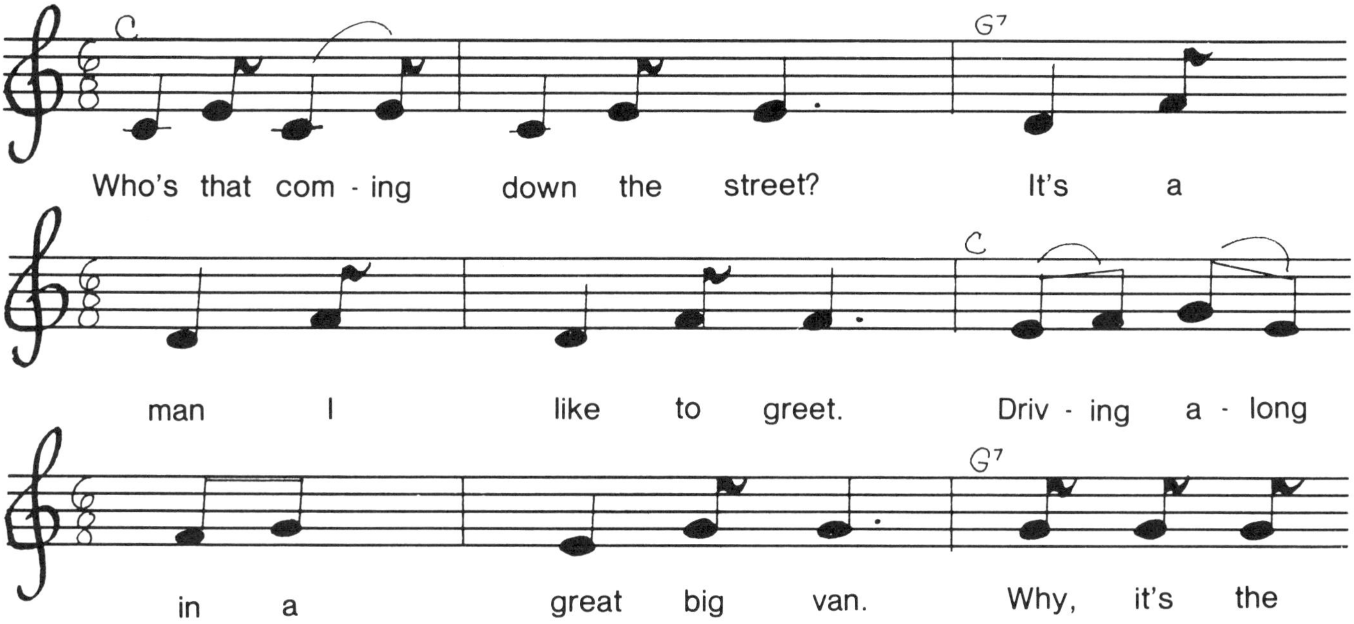

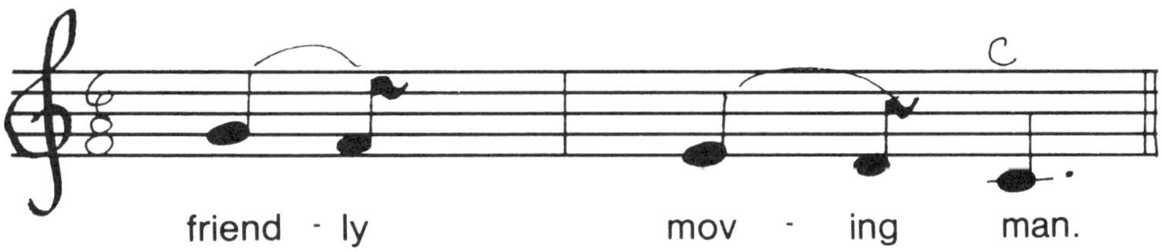

Give the new child in the classroom individual attention in order to ease his fears.

Read an appropriate book or talk about the fears children have about moving from one area to another. Share personal stories which show the humorous side of moving.

Plan to move one of the classroom centers from one section of the room to another. Assist the children in planning the move, packing and transferring each item of the center in a careful way.

The Farmer

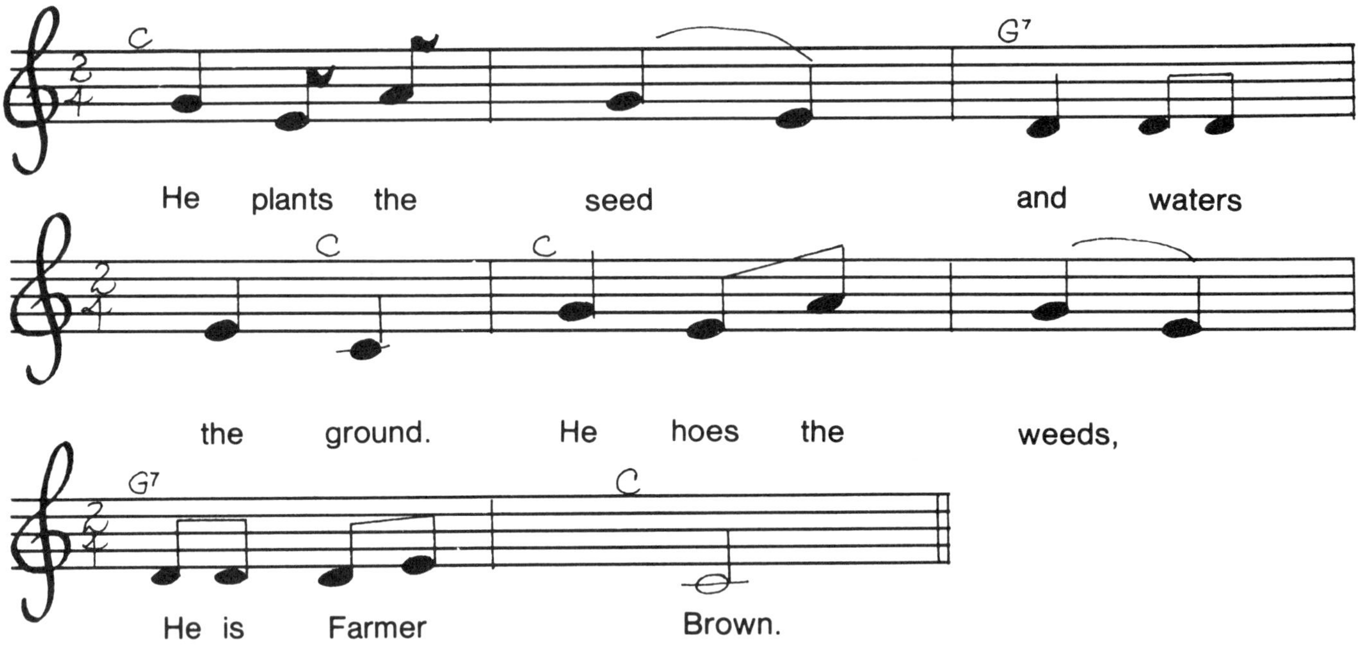

Plan a playground garden using seeds which will grow rapidly.

Select a child each day to be "Farmer Brown." This child's responsibility will include checking the plants and watering them, if needed.

Second Verse:

The tiny seedlings
Are growing so tall.
Then Farmer Brown
Harvests in the fall.

The Fireman

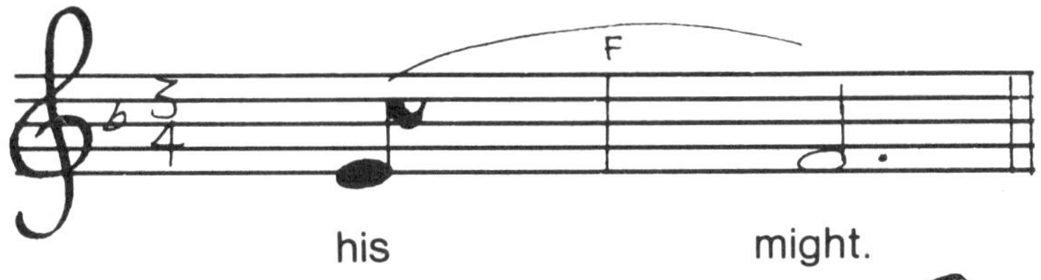

Visit the fire station in the community. Ask the fireman to demonstrate as much of his equipment as possible.

Talk about fire safety rules. Have a fire drill early in the year so the children will know the procedure to follow in case of fire.

The Baker

Visit a bakery. Ask parents to send money with the children so they can buy a freshly baked cookie.

Have a cooking lesson in class where children can help in the preparation. A number of nonbake recipes are available.

The Astronaut

Select a book which describes what an astronaut is, his training and his mission.

Purchase a jar of Tang, the breakfast drink of astronauts, and serve during snack time.

The Grocer

Plan a trip to a neighborhood grocery store so each child can buy a canned vegetable he likes. Return to the school and prepare macaroni in a large pot adding the vegetables the children have purchased. Discuss why this recipe is called "Friendship Soup." Have plastic-coated paper bowls ready so everyone in the class can sample the soup. Invite another group of children in the school to share in the fun.

TRANSPORTATION

A natural accompaniment to a study of community helpers is a study of transportation. All citizens of any community setting will need to use some form of transportation at one time or another. Firemen use fire trucks, policemen use police cars, pilots use jets, and newsboys use bicycles. Any busy street is testimony to the ever-increasing mobility of today's society.

A trip by car is a normal everyday occurrence. Most preschoolers have even traveled by bus, train or plane. Hot wheels, hot cycles, tricycles and wagons are available to the child who fancies such items as toys. Class discussions about transportation, murals, field trips and role playing will add depth to use of the songs presented in this section.

Suggested concepts to use in this section include:

* There are many means of transportations.
* People travel on land, on sea and in the air.
* Traffic signs and transportation help provide safety for citizens.
* Some transportation means are public and others are privately owned.
* Children have responsibilities to adults when they are operating vehicles.

SONGS:

The Jet

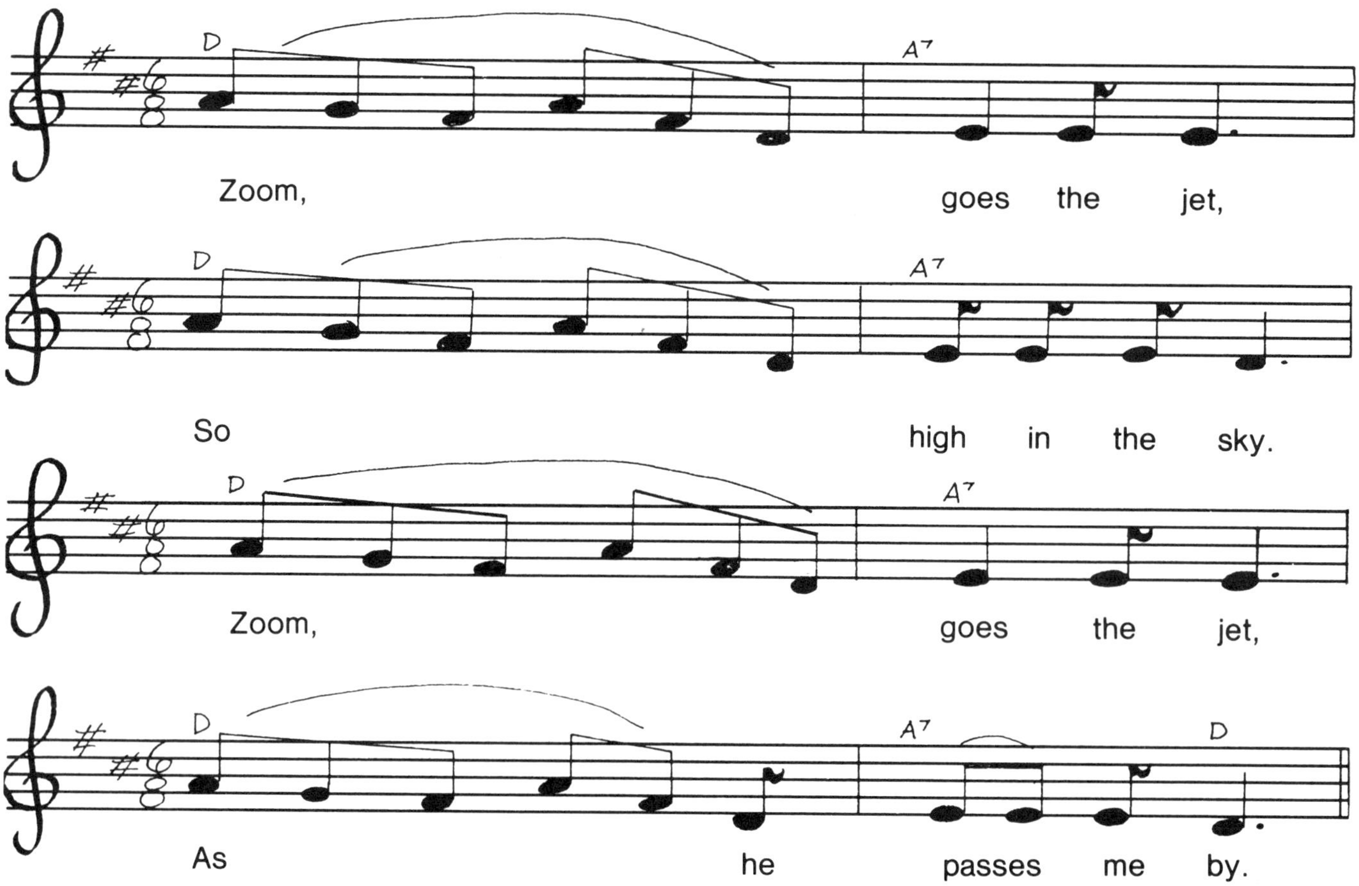

Move around the room with arms extended like the jet's wings. To prevent confusion, precede the activity with instruction to children about avoiding collisions with other "jets."

The Train

Form a line of children to represent the train. Show them how to use shuffling motions with their feet and locomotor-type movements with their arms to move around the room as they sing the song.

After the children know the song well, choose one child to sing the third phrase of the song as if he were the conductor.

The Car

Discuss different sounds cars make. A tape of various sounds could be played for identification (starting the engine, locking doors, brakes squealing, horn blowing, car door shutting, radio playing, windshield wipers moving, car moving, flashers clicking, gears shifting, etc.).

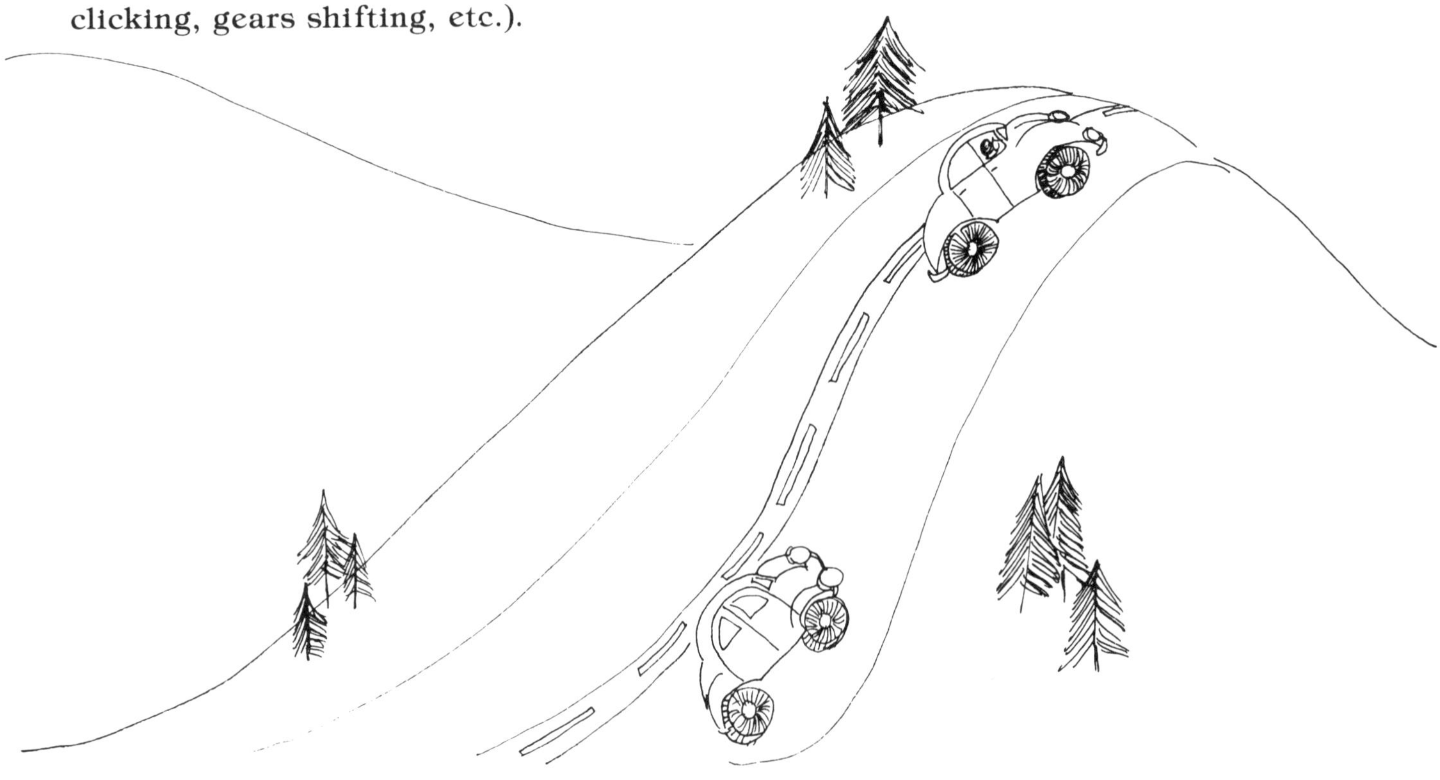

Taxi!

Paint a transportation mural and display in the room. Divide the mural in half with the top part blue for the sky and the bottom part brown. Individual children may draw and cut out cars to represent taxis. At a later time, add other vehicles which are used in the air or on the ground.

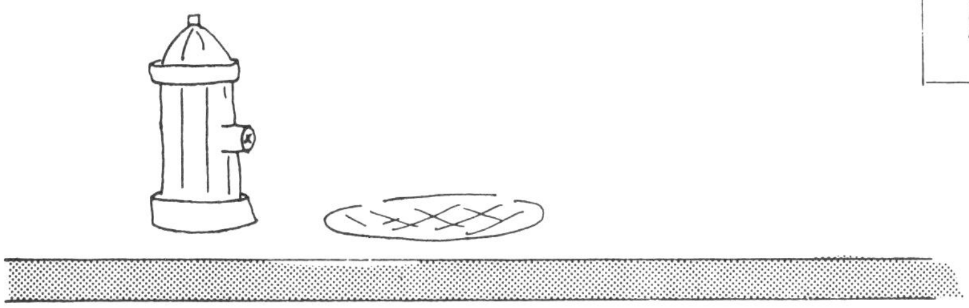

Rowing My Boat

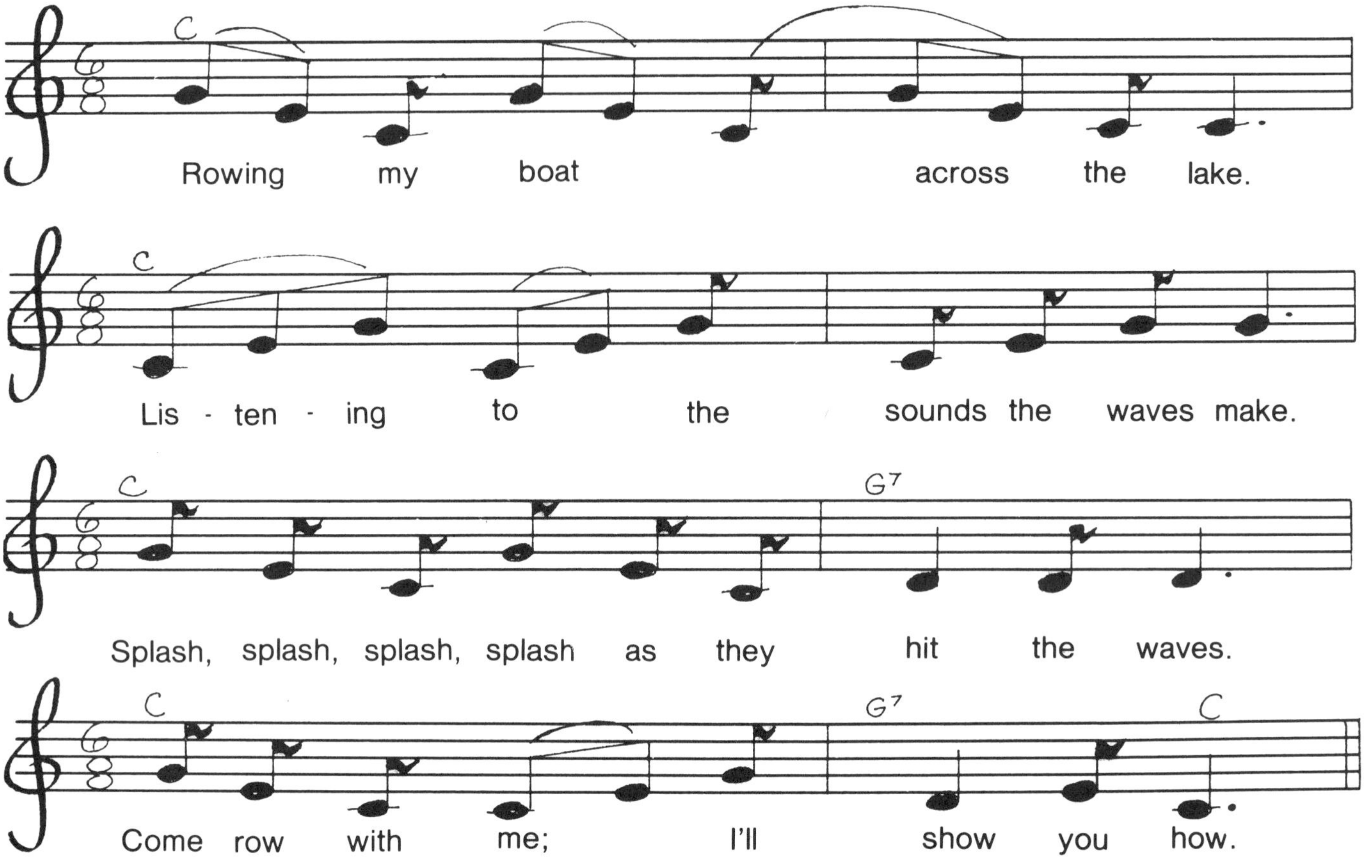

Make cork boats with paper sails. Ivory soap or sponges make boats, also. Correlate this activity with a discussion of what sinks or floats.

Teach children to "row" a boat by sitting down back-to-back. Join arms at the elbows to get a true feel for the rowing motion.

Bus

Most field trip experiences automatically include trips on buses. Before any trip, secure permission slips signed by parents and emphasize bus safety with the children.

An excellent field trip idea is to plan a bus trip to visit the community airport.

Crossing the Street

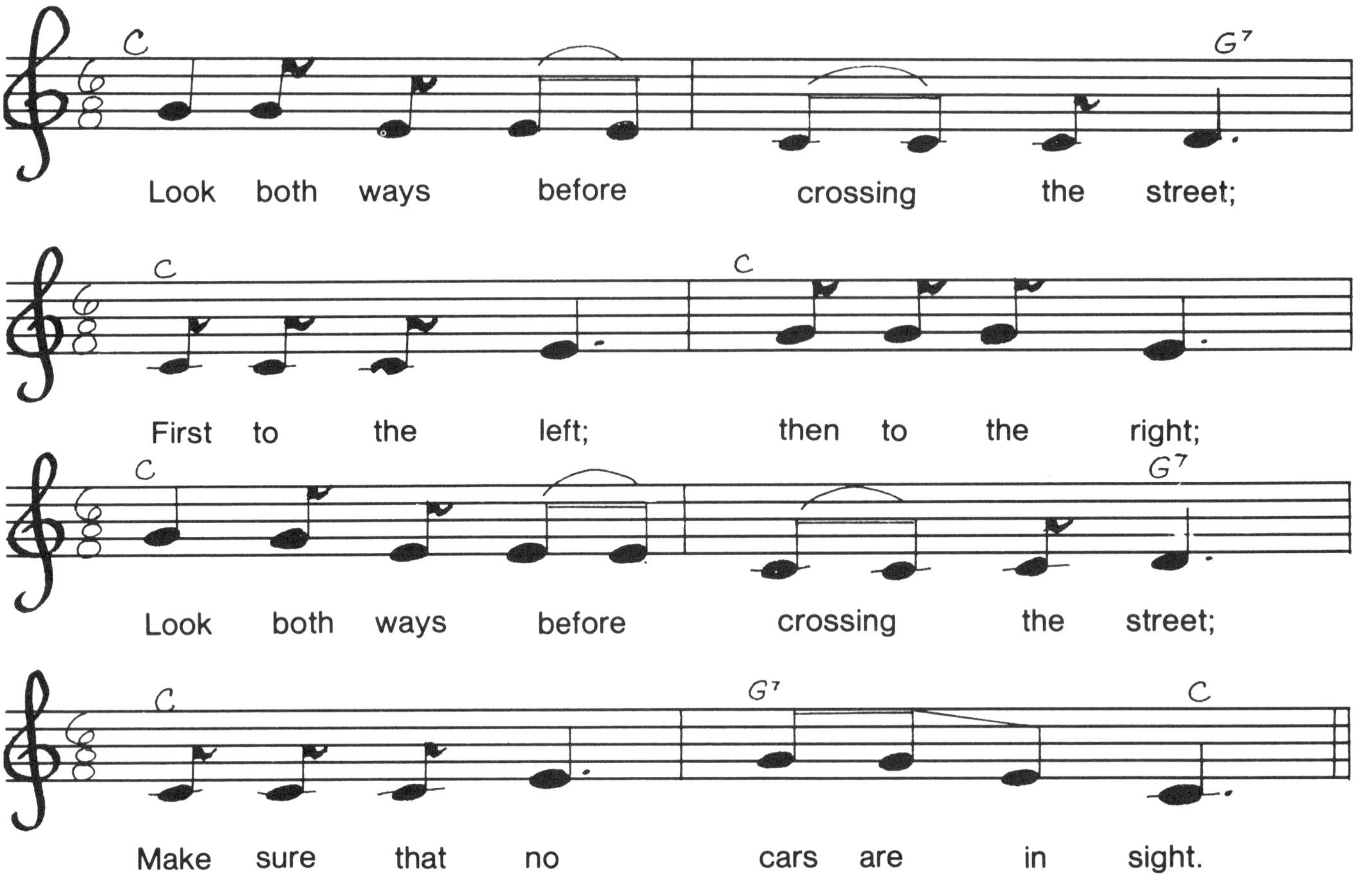

Set up teacher-made or commercial traffic signs at several places in the classroom. Play a Follow-the-Leader game to teach children to recognize common signs.

Practice crossing an intersection and sing the song to reinforce correct procedures.

Provide appropriate travel vehicles for children to use during creative play. Use large boxes painted to represent various vehicles. Use the boxes to set up traffic situations that children might encounter.

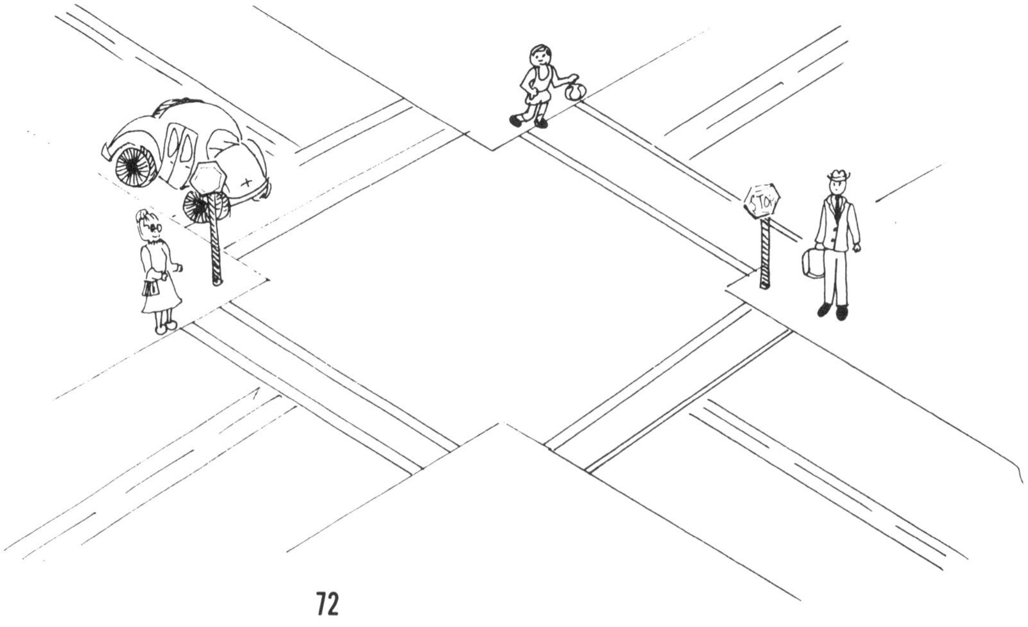

ANIMALS, INSECTS AND BIRDS

An adult's encounter with a small child will only make more clear the belief that children hold different views of the world. A youngster finds immense pleasure in observing an insect, for example, at close range and then proclaiming gleefully, "It leaped," as the insect moves about its daily living tasks. Some children are most apt at spotting a bird or animal long before the adults around them are aware that these creatures are in range.

The fascination children enjoy with animals, birds and insects is important in the classroom environment, too. Children will capture insects, snakes or butterflies and bring them to share with their peers. Watching a caterpillar weave its cocoon or ants build a home are excellent science lessons which teacher will want children to experience. Capturing the interest of the children will not be difficult to manage.

Suggested concepts to be developed in this section include:

* Animals make different sounds.
* Animals live in different environments.
* Some animals are domestic; others live in the wild.
* Animals serve man in different capacities.

SONGS:

Bees

A teacher-made glove puppet (see page 75) can effectively enhance the singing of this song. The children who do not have puppets can fold their thumbs and fingers into a fist to represent a hive as they sing "one, two, three, four, five" in the song.

“Buzzing Bee” Glove Puppet

Color bees black and yellow and wear on a black glove.

Butterfly, Fly

Attach a butterfly pattern to a dowel rod to make a stick puppet. Move the puppets in time to the music.

Butterfly Stick Puppet

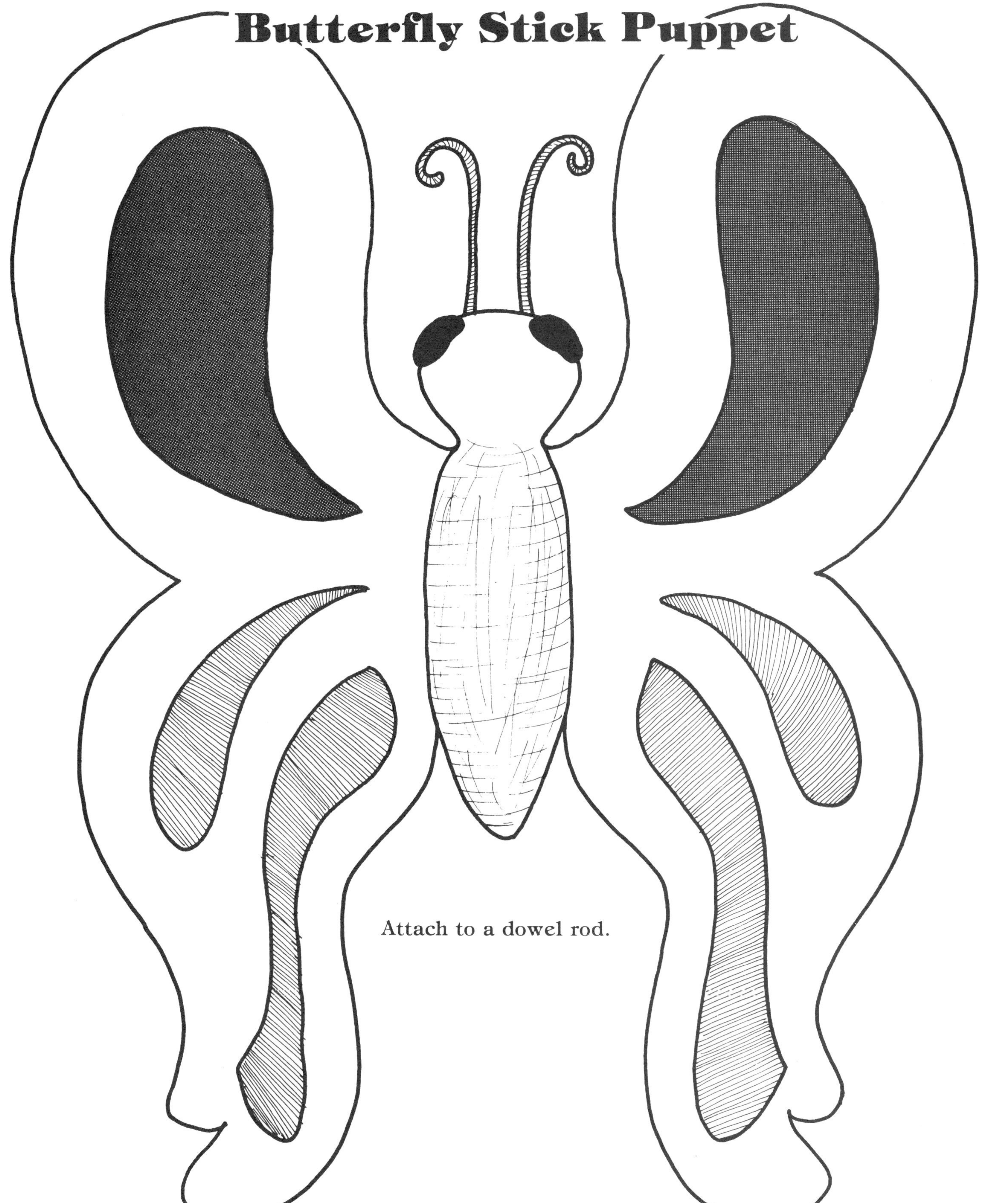

The Owl

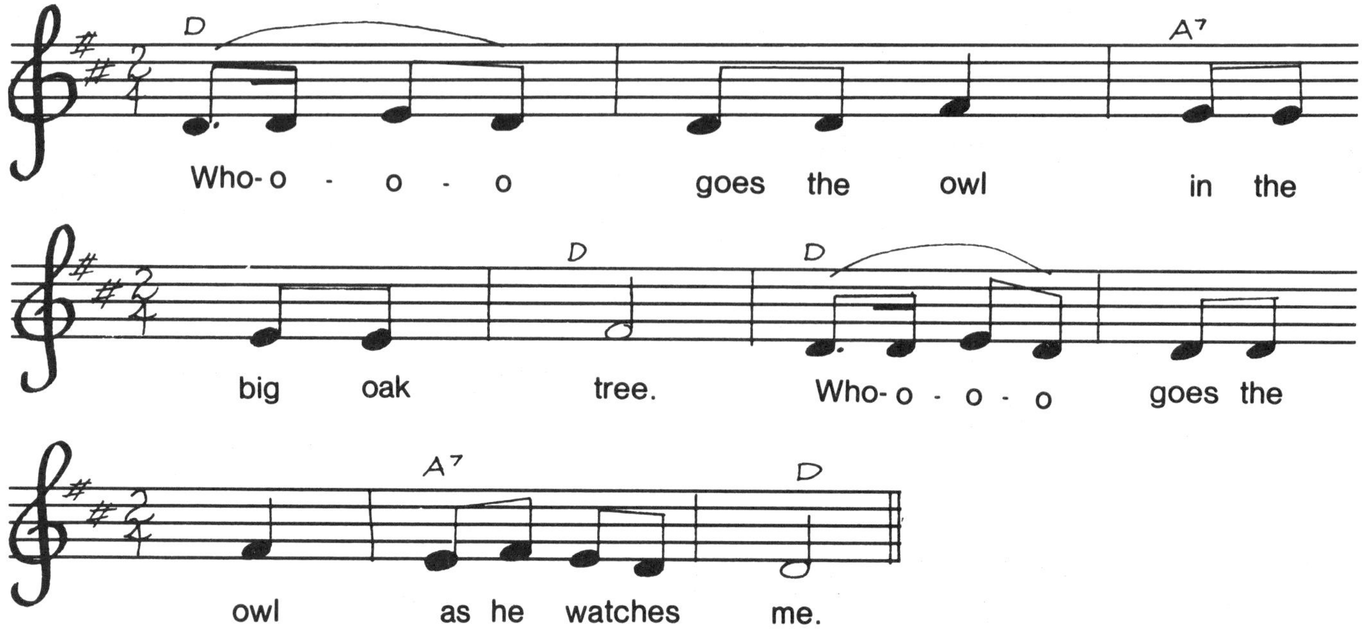

Have animal, insect, and bird sounds recorded on tape for the children to identify.

Listen carefully to hear the owl's hoot.

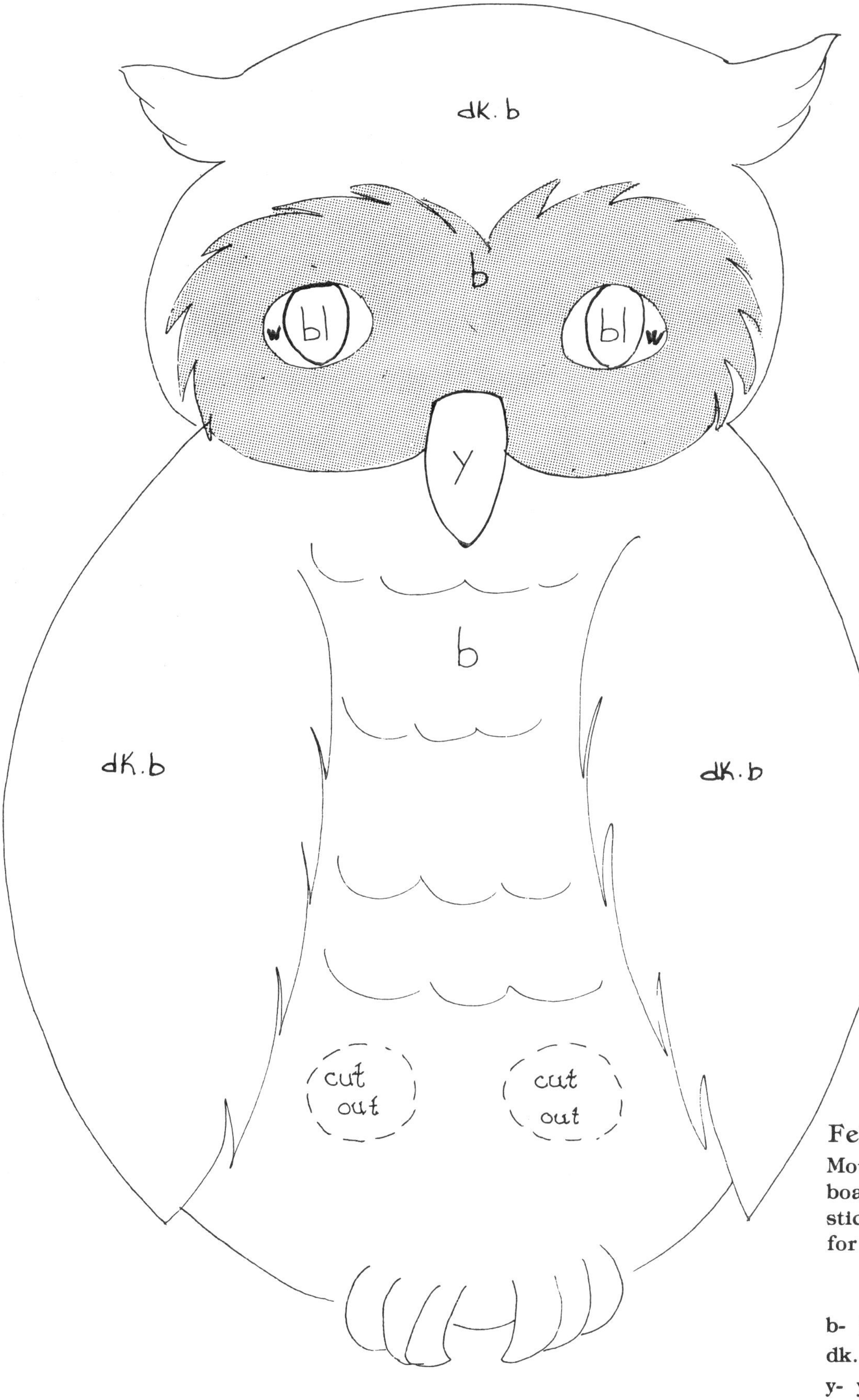

Felt Owl Puppet

Mount onto cardboard and attach a stick or cut holes for fingers.

Color key:

b- beige
dk. b- dark brown
y- yellow
bl- black
w- white

Farm Sounds

Play a guessing game to go with "Farm Sounds" song. Let the children take turns making an animal sound for his classmates to guess which animal is being imitated.

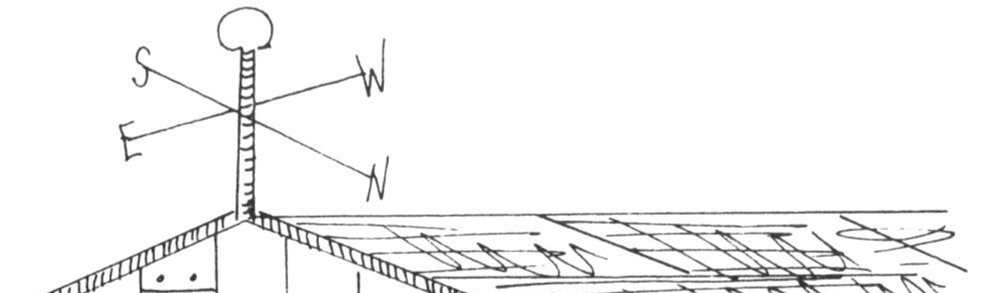

Oink, Oink

Discuss the difference between what is real and what is make-believe. For example, ask the children such questions as "Can animals talk?" or "Can we talk with a pig or a horse?"

Have several picture cards in the manipulatives center showing pictures of pigs of various sizes. Children can put the pictures in order from **largest** pig to **smallest** pig (or **fattest** pig to **skinniest** pig).

The Monkey

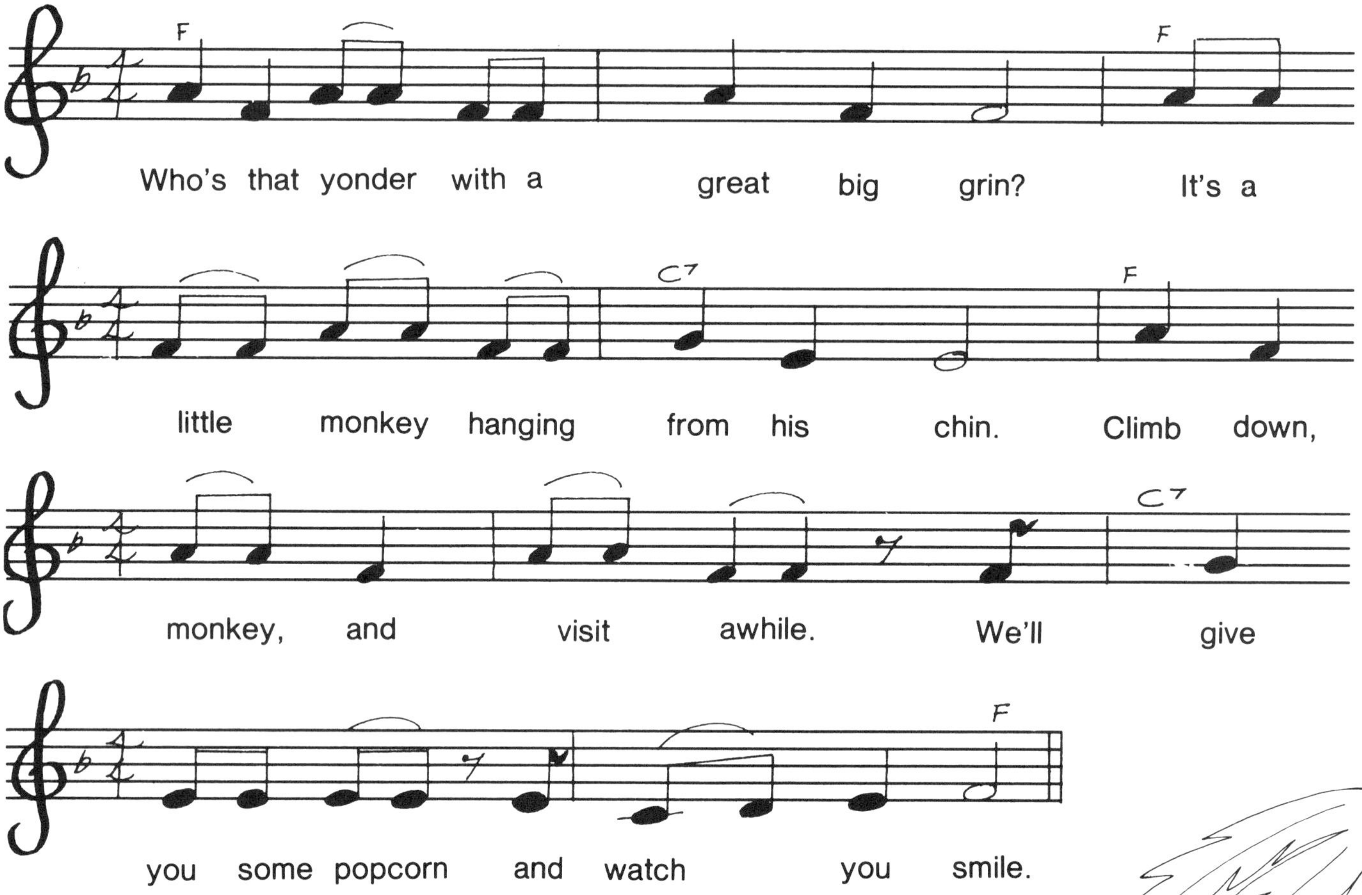

Make up motions to go with this song. Children will delight in doing some creative thinking for themselves as they experiment with motions.

Down in the Meadow

Take a field trip through a wooded area, along a beach, in a meadow or whatever is appropriate in the area. Look at the wildlife.

Using a large chart and pictures of animals, let children classify animals into categories (such as animals in air or on land, domestic or wild, farm, zoo, forest or jungle animals).

Guess the Animal (Giraffe)

Guess the giraffe's name.

Guess the Animal (Camel)

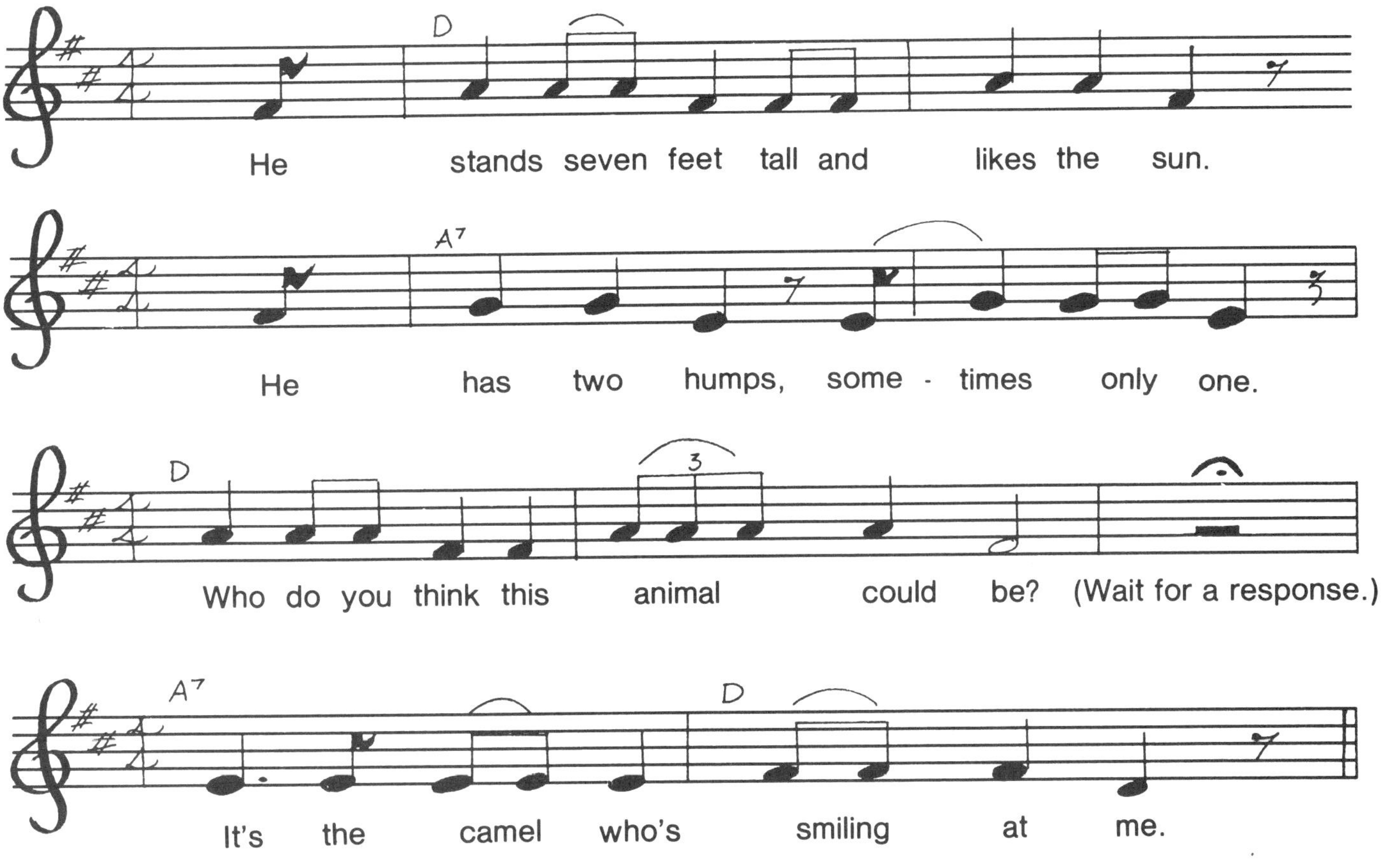

Guess the camel's name.

Guess the Animal (Turtle)

Guess the turtle's name.

Guess the Animal (Penguin)

Guess the penguin's name.

The Birds

Talk about the shape of birds with the class, and let each child create a bird using construction paper and feathers purchased at a hobby shop. Hang the birds from the ceiling or a wire which is strung across the room.

COUNTING SONGS

Counting is an integral part of the young child's early experiences. It seems that children begin acquiring concepts about "oneness," "twoness," or "threeness" even as they begin to learn their first words. The songs in this section serve to expand and extend the child's knowledge about numbers. To be truly effective, the teacher needs to concentrate on making every encounter with numerical concepts a concrete experience. Manipulating objects or moving one's body in some fashion gives far more satisfaction than just saying or singing the words. A wise teacher will observe very carefully to determine if the child is knowledgable about number concepts or is merely saying the words.

Suggested concepts to be developed in this section include:

* Numbers follow an ordered sequence.
* One-to-one correspondence can be illustrated through simple counting songs.
* There is a correlation between verbal symbols and written symbols.
* Man uses counting skills to determine how many or how much of a thing exists.

SONGS:

Ten Little Flowers

Dramatize the action of the flowers in the song "Ten Little Flowers." The first ten children can be chosen by the teacher. These children can choose the next ten "flowers."

Ten Pretty Seagulls

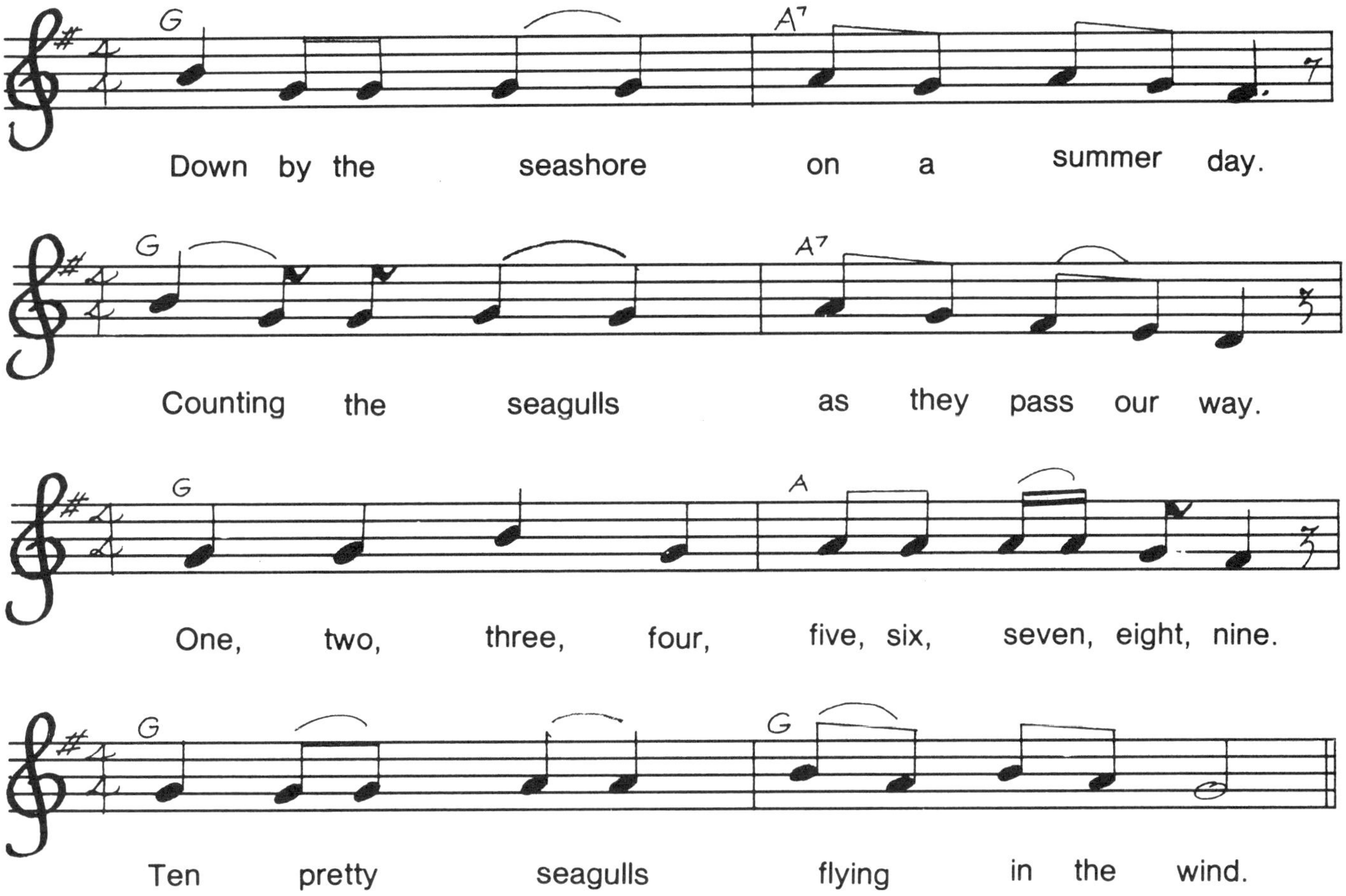

Count ten precut felt seagulls which are displayed on a flannel board while singing the song.

Baby Chicks

While singing the song "Baby Chicks," the children can close their hands to hide the chicks. As they count the chicks, the children unfold hands and hold up fingers.

I Can Count to Eight

Do the motions described in this song. Touch eight different parts of the body as the counting section of the song is recited. See how many new body parts can be added as the song is sung a second and third time.

Body Numbers

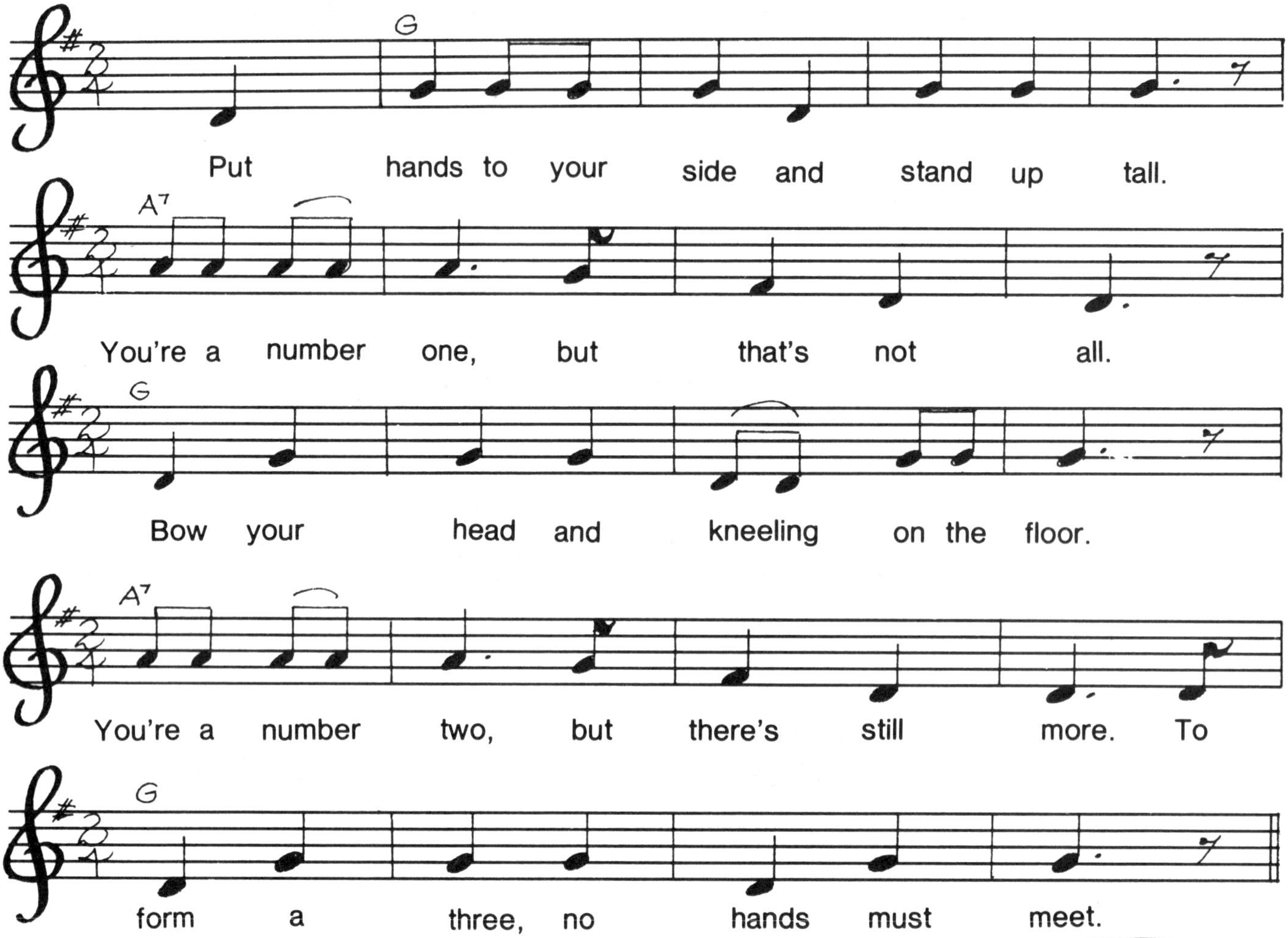

Follow the instructions in the song to form the numerals as they are described. To facilitate proper musical timing, ask children to be in one of the body positions before the song is sung. Sing.

Body Numbers

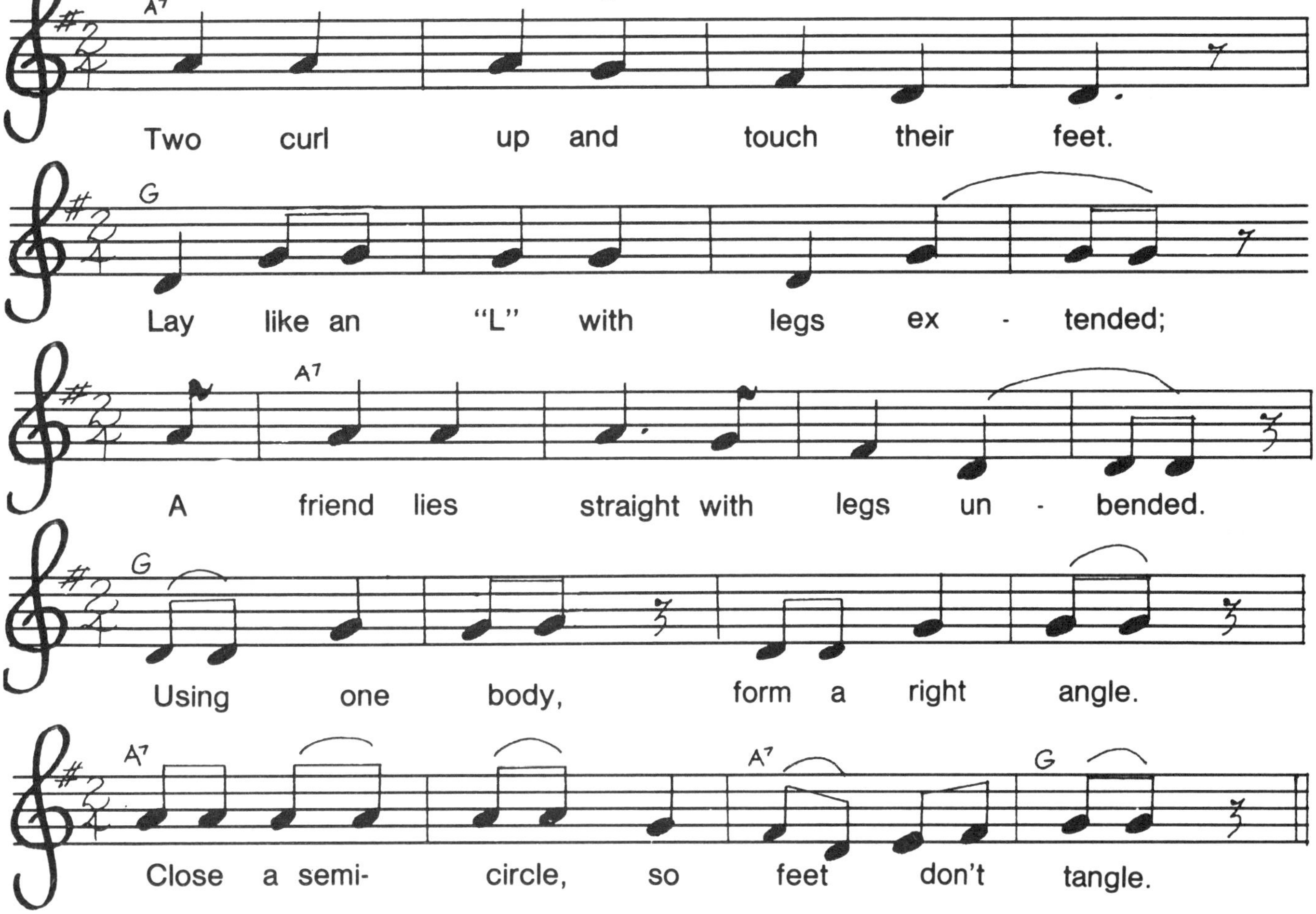

Sing the song several times and suggest to the children that they try more than one position. In several instances, children will need to work in pairs in order to make the numerals.

Counting Song

Ask children to count out any eight objects they wish to use to serve as props when singing this song. Suggest finding pebbles, twigs, leaves, pine cones or other items on the playground.

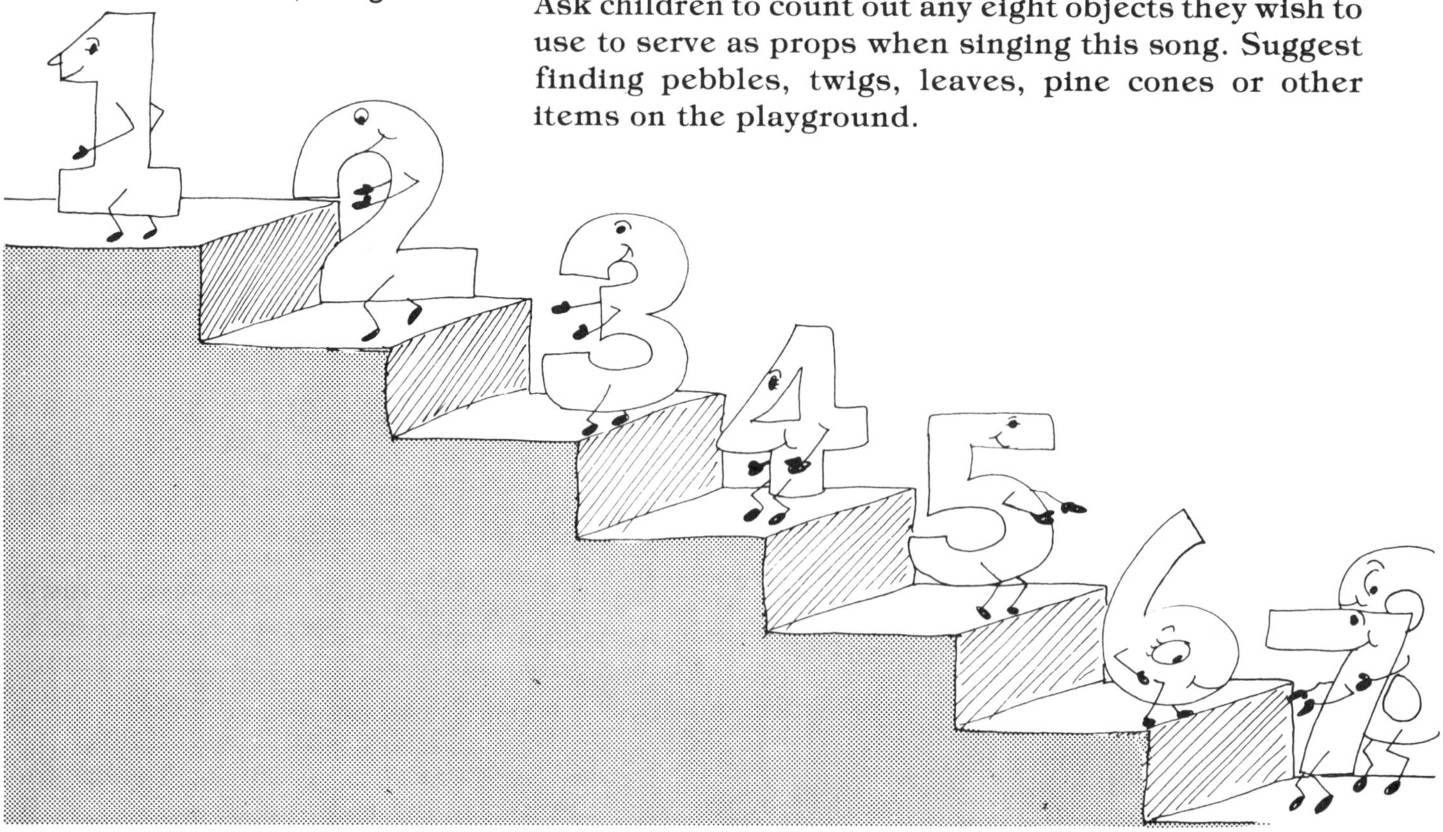

Let's March

Form a long line and march while this song is sung. At another time, provide materials for children to make flags to use when they march.

JUST FOR FUN

The songs included in this section of the book have defied classification. Most of them are appropriate for areas of study in the preschool, and many will be used over and over again. However, they did not appear to "fit" other categories previously listed. It is anticipated that these songs indeed may be used "just for fun."

SONGS:

Stars

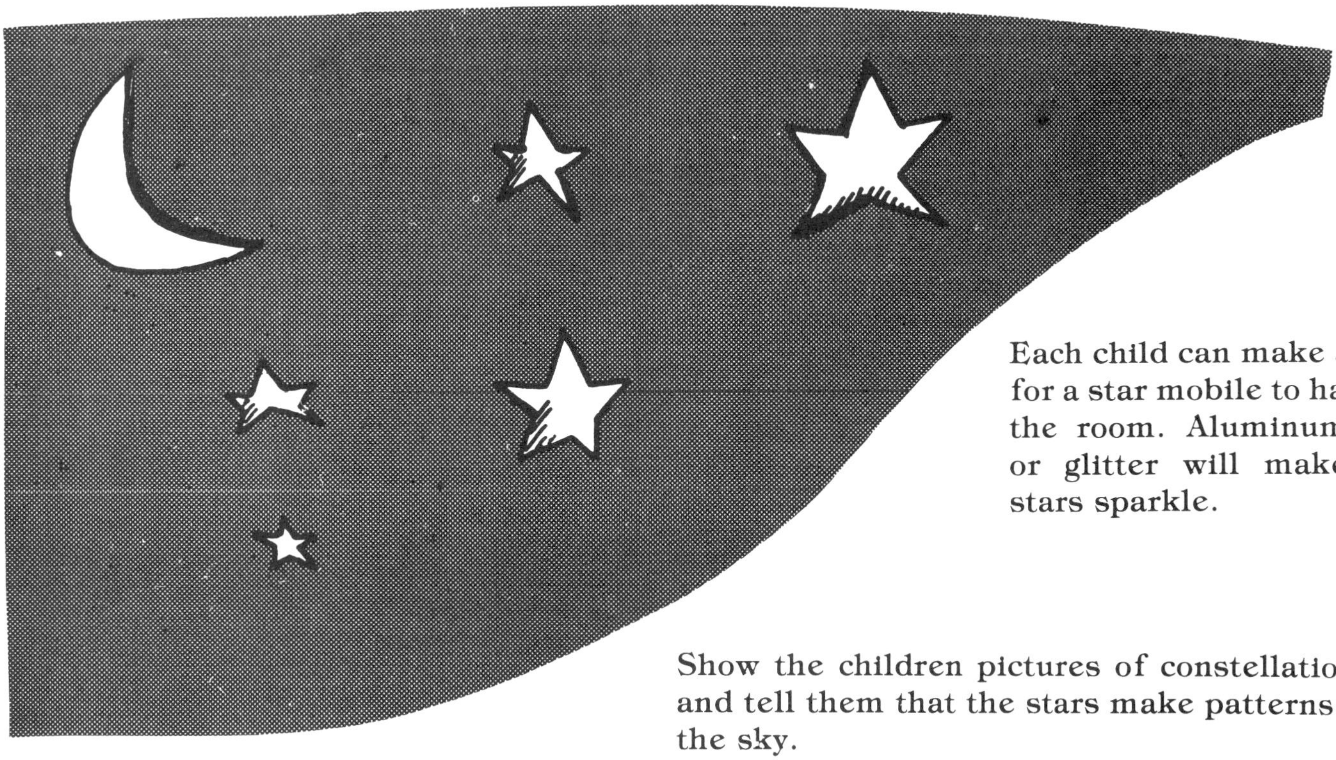

Each child can make a star for a star mobile to hang in the room. Aluminum foil or glitter will make the stars sparkle.

Show the children pictures of constellations and tell them that the stars make patterns in the sky.

The Brass Band

Invite high school band students to come to school and introduce brass instruments to the children. Community symphony groups may also be contacted to provide ensembles.

Making Music

Have children make a musical instrument such as a coffee can drum or paper plate castanets. Form a classroom band and let each child play his instrument.

Change the words **banjo** and **drum** to name other musical instruments. Remember to change **plink** and **bum,** too. Children will enjoy experimenting with onomatopoeic variations.

Funny Little Clown

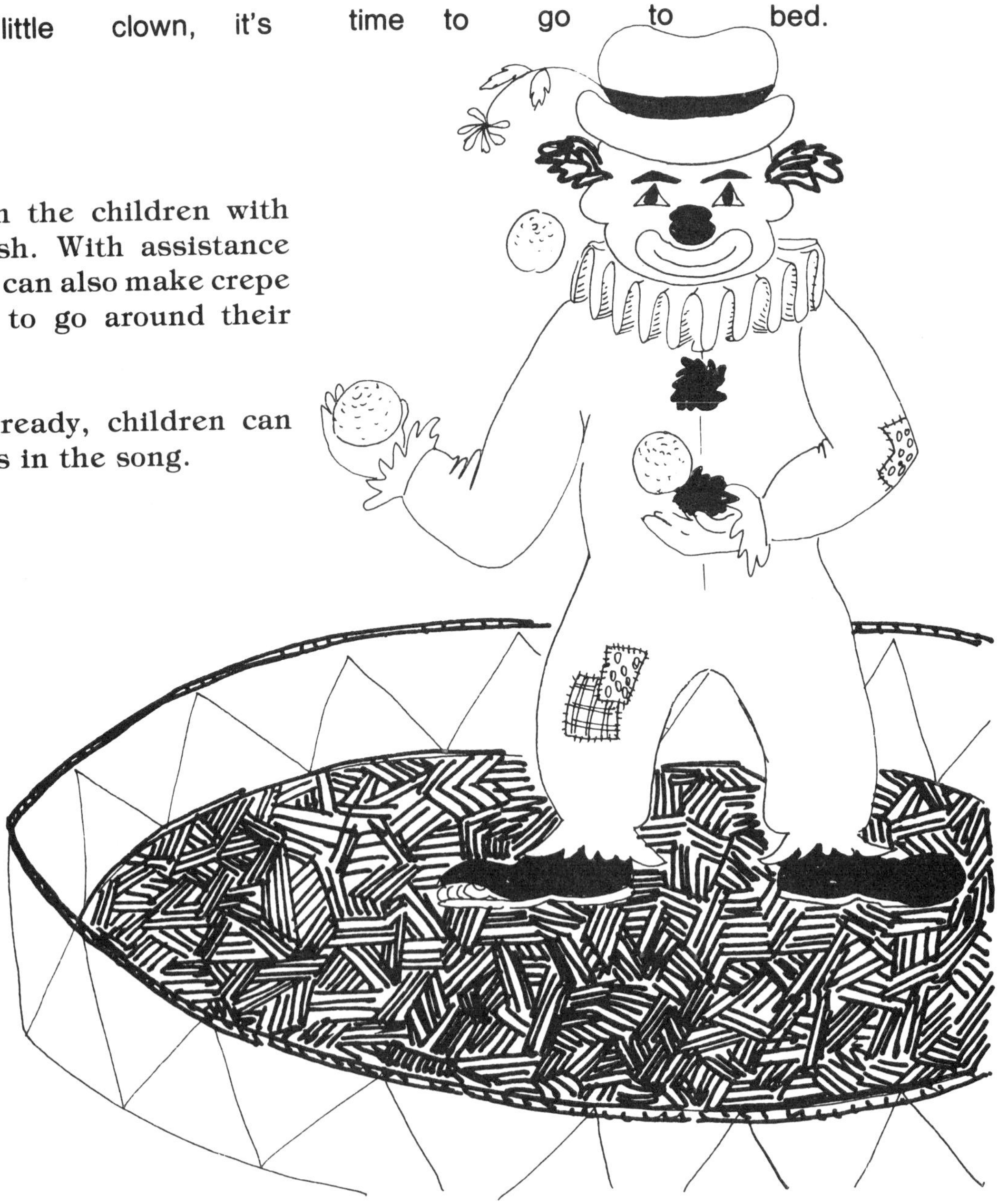

Paint clown faces on the children with watercolors and brush. With assistance from adults, children can also make crepe paper clown ruffles to go around their necks.

Once costumes are ready, children can dramatize the actions in the song.

The Seashore

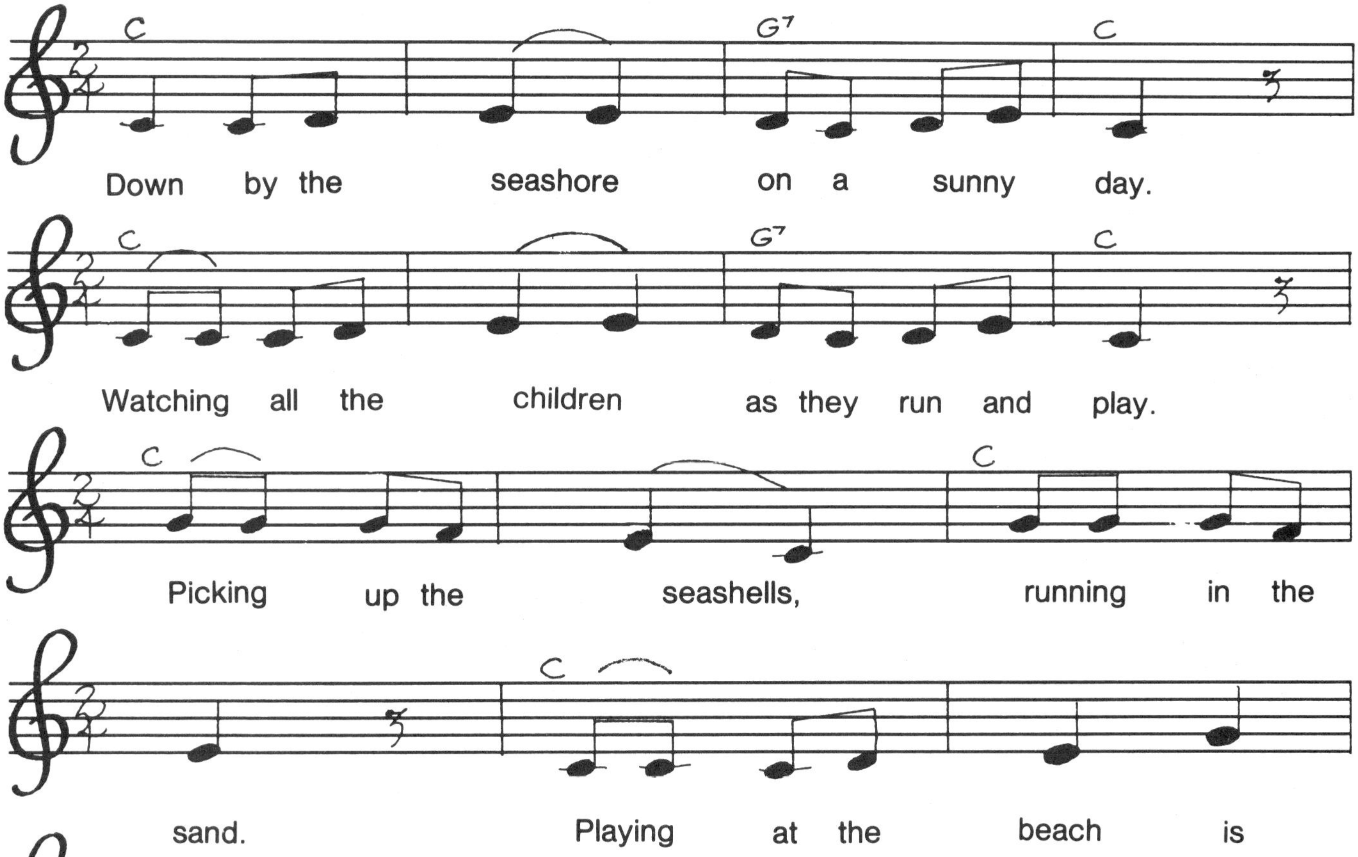

Discuss the sounds of the seashore. Listen to a shell and hear the ocean roar. Visit a seashore if possible and collect shells.

Make a seashell collage.

Collect large shells to use to make dried flower arrangements. Center florist clay in the shells and add dried flowers to form a bouquet. These make lovely gifts.

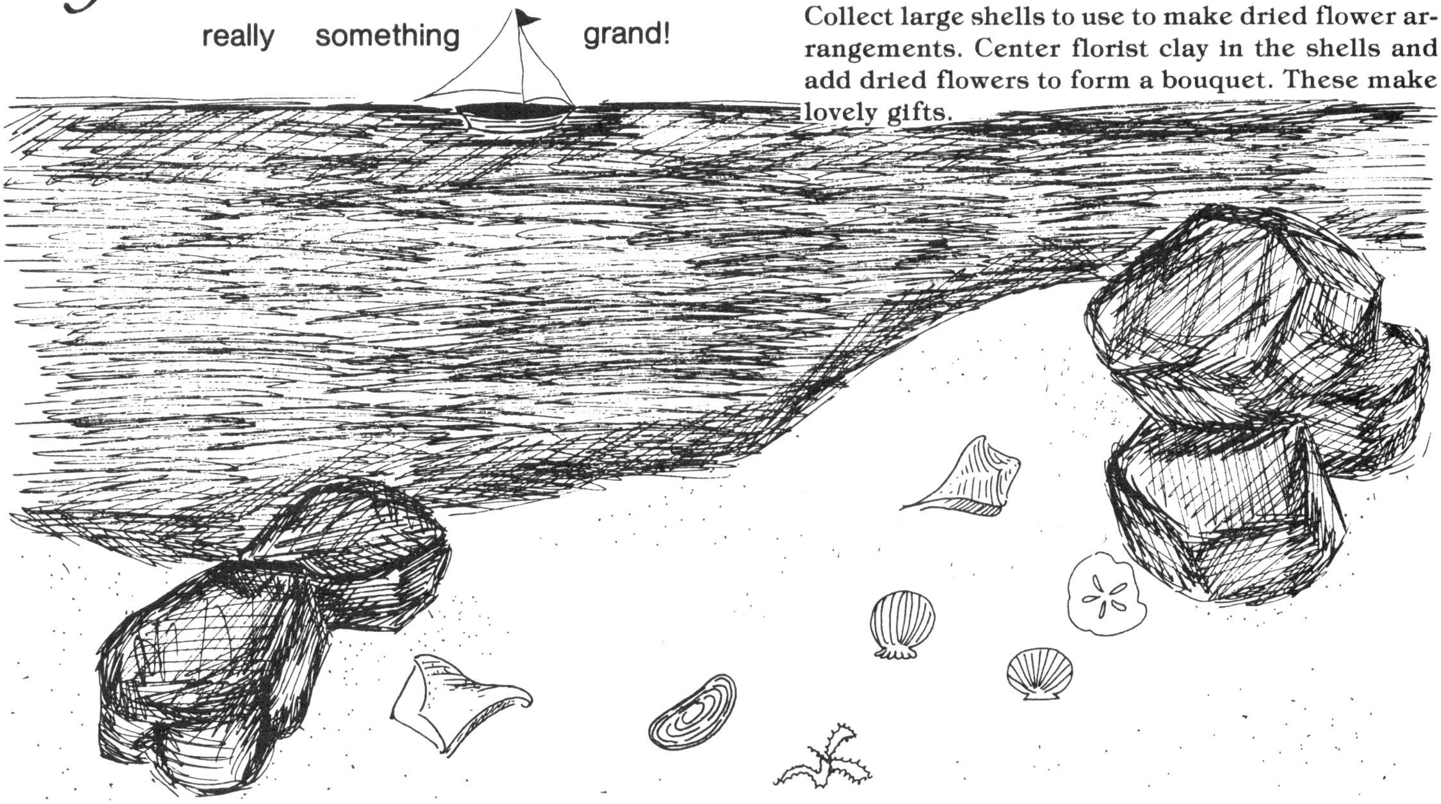

Clap With Me

Clap simultaneously when singing the word **clap** on the last four measures.

Suggest variations in the song by changing the word **clap,** to **hop, snap, pat, nod, jump,** etc. Allow the children to make suggestions of their own.

INDEX OF SONGS